KATACHI

JAPANESE PATTERN
AND DESIGN IN
WOOD, PAPER, AND CLAY

KATACHI

JAPANESE PATTERN
AND DESIGN IN
WOOD, PAPER, AND CLAY

Photographs by Takeji Iwamiya

Introductory Essay by Donald Richie

WEIDENFELD AND NICOLSON

20 NEW BOND STREET LONDON W1

© 1963 Harry N. Abrams, Incorporated, New, York, N.Y.

Produced by Bijutsu Shuppan-Sha, Tokyo

Photographic layout by Yoshio Hayakawa

Printed and bound in Japan

CONTENTS

MAN IS THE ONLY ONE among the animals to make patterns, and among men, the Japanese are probably the foremost makers of patterns. They are a patterned people who live in a patterned country, a land where habit is exalted to rite, where the exemplar still exists, where there is a model for everything and the ideal is actively sought, where the shape of an idea or an action may be as important as its content, where the configuration of parts depends upon recognized form, and the profile of the country depends upon the shape of living.

The profile is visible—to think of Japan is to think of form. But beneath this, a moral pattern exists. There is a way to pay calls, a way to go shopping, a way to drink tea, a way to arrange flowers, a way to owe money. A formal absolute exists and is aspired to; social form must be satisfied if social chaos is to be avoided. Though others have certain small rituals that give the disordered flux of life a kind of order, here these become an art of behavior. It is reflected in the language, a tongue where the cliché is expected; there is a formal phrase for meeting and for parting, and for begging pardon, for expressing sorrow, for showing anger, surprise, love itself.

This attachment to pattern is expressed in other ways: Japan is one of the last countries to wear costumes. Not only the fireman and the policeman, but also the student and the laborer. There is a suit for hiking, a costume for striking; there is the unmistakable fashion for the boy who belongs to a gang and the indubitable ensemble of the fallen woman. In old Japan, the pattern was even more apparent; a fishmonger wore this, a vegetable seller, that; a samurai had his uniform as surely as the geisha had hers. The country should have resembled one of those picture scrolls of famous gatherings in which everyone was plainly labeled, or one of those formal games—the chess-like shogi of which the Japanese are so fond—in which each piece is marked and is capable of so much power, each moving in a predetermined way, each known, each recognizable.

More than the Arabs, more than the Chinese, the Japanese feel the need for pattern and, hence, impose it. Confucius with his code of behavior lives on in Japan, not in China; the Japanese would probably have embraced the rigorous Koran had they known about it. This is the country where the pleasant custom of afternoon tea becomes the austere ritual of the *chanoyu.*

The triumph of form is, however, mainly visual. Ritual is disturbed by the human; spontaneity ruins ethics. The musical, the culinary, the literary art are rudimentary and observe only the general rule of custom. Japan makes patterns for the eyes, and names are remembered only if read. Hearing is fallible; the eye is sure. Japan is the country of calling cards and forests of advertising; it is also the country of the camera and the amateur artist. Everyone can draw, everyone can take pictures. Visual composition is not taught; it is known; it is like having perfect pitch.

To make a pattern is to discover and copy it; a created form presumes an archetype. In Japan, one suffers none of the claustrophobia of the Arab countries—geometrical wildernesses—none of the horror of America—the kaleidoscope come full stop—because the model for the patterns and designs of Japan is nature itself.

From the air, always a good introduction to the patterns of a country, Japan is all paddies winding in free-form serpentine between mountain and valley, a quilt of checks and triangles, more like Italy—another country where nature remains the norm—and different from the neat squares of Germany—so much for so many—and the vast and regular checkerboard of America. The Japanese pattern is drawn from nature, and the paddy fields assume their shape because mountains are observed and valleys are followed, because this is the country where the house is made to fit comfortably into the curve of the landscape, where the farmer cuts a hole in his roof rather than cut down a tree, and where the beautiful is the natural.

The merely natural, however, is never beautiful enough. Wordsworth would dislike the country, so would Byron. That nature is grand only when it is completely natural would never occur to a Japanese. The ideal is that of the eighteenth century, an ordered landscape, and Chippendale would have been Japanese had he only known. Forests become parks; trees are dwarfed; living flowers are arranged. One does not go against nature, but one takes advantage of it; one smooths, one embellishes. Nature is only the potential, man gives it its shape and meaning.

Since it is the natural forms that are traditionally most admired—the single rock, the spray of bamboo—it is these which are seen most frequently in Japanese art, delivered from the chaotic context of nature and given meaning through their isolation. There are canons, but they are close to nature's own. Purple and red do not clash because, since they occur often enough in nature, no law of color can suggest that their proximity is unsatisfying. A single branch set at one side of the nichelike tokonoma and balanced by nothing is not ill-composed because there is a rule that insists that formal balance is necessarily good. The Japanese garden is not the French; symmetry is something imposed upon nature, not drawn from it; asymmetry is a compromise between regularity and chaos.

Thus, Japan's vocabulary of images, the iconography of the country, is drawn from natural forms, and this creates a consistent style that occurs in gardens, parks, temples, houses, cups and saucers—repeated, stressed, made uniform—a vision of the natural imposed upon the visible world. At times, the artifact is almost indistinguishable from the original—the artificial rock, the man-made vista. Often the object—a stone, a tree—becomes the pretext for an extended scene. Just as the true Japanese religion is animistic—a religion of shapes, first the strange rock, the riven tree is discovered, then the temple or shrine grows. First the form, then the content—the watchful god. So, the patterns and designs of Japan revert continually to an ideal, to a shape sometimes only imagined and not shown, to a form sometimes defined only by what surrounds it—to a satisfying ideal first glimpsed in nature and now brought forth.

The pillar, the standing form. The Japanese house—roof built first, walls last—hangs upon it; it stands like a tree in the center, and though it may be planed, it is never painted. In other countries the pillar becomes Trajan's Column, the Eiffel Tower, Washington's Momument, but in Japan it is kept small, its origins unobscured. It is the hidden pillar base *(page 5)*, the standing support unhidden because it is necessary *(page 24)*; it is lintel *(page 26)* and decoration *(page 6)*; it is grave marker *(page 37, lower right)* and pincushion *(pages 46, 51)* and toy *(page 67)*. It takes a strong civilization—the Greek, the Roman, the nineteenth-century American—to use the column for itself, for its own sake; less direct cultures hide their columns. It takes Japan to scale down the mighty standing form to hand size, to refuse the aggrandizement that pillars as well as spires give, to adapt the mountain and the tree to human needs, to tame and domesticate this most recalcitrant of forms.

In the West, the high, standing form is sometimes most insisted upon; but in Asia, the form most prized is the round, the flat: lakes, pools, the ocean itself, caves, terraces upon which the flattened buildings squat. It is no accident that the national flower of Japan should be the Imperial Chrysanthemum *(pages 8–9, 29)*, just as France's flower must necessarily be the baroque fleur-de-lis and the Scots should find meaning and beauty in the thistle. Like the peony *(page 15)*, the chrysanthemum creates the round fullness that the Chinese and the Japanese have found rewarding. If the pillar supports the house, then the common round rice bucket *(page 81)* supports the family.

But just as the Japanese make the standing form useful and accessible, so the perfectly round is found too regular. Though the Japanese are as fond of the abstract perfection of the circle, the continuous curved line, the yin-and-yang design *(pages 28, 32, 151)*, as are the Chinese, in practice it is nature and not geometry that is followed. The circle is pulled, the ideal is suggested, nature is satisfied; the bell shape *(pages 7, 103)* or its obverse *(page 11)* is achieved. The peach is the most beautiful of fruit *(page 20)*; the temple gong *(page 93)* reflects its contours; even trees are clipped to suggest it *(page 145)*; in fenestration *(page 157)*, it permeates Japanese design. The great Buddhist teacher, Daruma, has been given this shape *(pages 66, 101, 108)*—he meditated so well that his limbs atrophied; that sleep might not interfere, he tore off his eyelids and threw them to the ground where they sprouted, in the shape of the familiar pointed oblong, and from them grew the tea plant whose leaves still retain this beloved form. The jealous goddess Benten, an importation from India, played the *biwa (pages 78–79)* and its form so ravished the Japanese that now so humble an object as a rice paddle *(pages 35, 81)* retains it, and provincial temples of the goddess show her not with her instrument but with the paddle, and from a goddess suspicious of lovers, she has become a matron watching benevolently over wayfarers and married couples.

Most countries insist upon the geometrical, design subdues nature. In the Islamic countries, everything not geometrical is excluded; in Greece alone, geometry becomes an art, and the rightness of the Parthenon insists upon the archetypical rectangle in the heart of each of us. Japan insists that this same geometry of the heart be reached through other means. We must observe nature. We must schematize it, then we must reconstruct it. One of the triumphs of Japanese perception is that the merely straight and the merely round are never enough—these two must exist by themselves in partial form, must be suggested, or they must be combined.

Of all patterns in Japan, the torii is the most Japanese: two uprights and a crosspiece creating, in the center, a square circle. It is a gate *(page 36)* or a door *(page 44)* or a tunnel *(page 2)*. No matter the use—window latticing *(pages 38, 39)*, building construction *(page 45)*, a clothes rack *(pages 47–49)*, an armrest *(page 54)*, or a stool *(pages 56–57)*—it is the union of the two major divisions of pattern and design, and it permeates the country: the entrance to the shrine of the temple, the entrance to the house, the shape itself of the tokonoma—it is both mountain and lake, forest and cave.

To think of Japan is to think of form—because these patterns are repeated often and faithfully. Wherever the eye rests they occur. They give the look of the land a consistency, as though a set of rules had been rigorously followed; these rules all unify the country, making it a bit more consistent than nature itself would be able, giving what usually identifies art—style.

It is these patterns, these shapes, these forms, these designs, occurring endlessly, which makes the country so satisfying to the eye, to the senses. Chaos, even now, is warded off, and pattern prevails. Man, to whom patterns are necessary, is satisfied; he lives with nature and is at peace.

DONALD RICHIE

x

A SUMMARY INTRODUCTION
TO THE CULTURAL HISTORY OF JAPAN

NARA PERIOD 710–793

This period marked the first true flowering of culture in Japan after the introduction of Buddhism from China two centuries earlier. The influence of the Chinese Tang Dynasty was extremely strong at Nara, the eighth-century capital of Japan. A steadily increasing flow of traffic between Japan and the mainland by Chinese scholars and teachers who brought their knowledge to Japan, and Japanese priests who went to China to learn, had impressed the influence of Chinese civilization on Japan. It had established Buddhism among the aristocrats of the capital of Nara, and had laid the basis for the later development of Japanese culture. The famous Todaiji, which was begun in 745 and dedicated in 752, is an expression of the strength of Chinese influence on Japanese architecture.

HEIAN PERIOD 794–1185

With the decline of the power and the subsequent disintegration of the Tang Dynasty between the later half of the eighth and the tenth centuries, the Chinese influence weakened. Japan began to create her own form of Buddhism as interpreted by Japanese priests, devised an indigenous alphabet, developed a system of laws and regulations suited to her own national circumstances, which resulted in the creation of a distinct and individual Japanese culture. However, the shrines and temples built during this period at Kyoto, the capital, continued to show the Chinese influence.

KAMAKURA PERIOD 1185–1333

Although Kyoto remained the capital, this period is marked by the emergence of the samurai—warrior—class in eastern Japan from a stronghold at Kamakura, from which this period takes its name. The court, the nobility, and the priests, who constituted the old power, and the samurai entered a long period of strife from which the samurai gradually emerged victorious. Kyoto was still the center of Japanese culture, but the life and ideals of the samurai were strongly reflected in it. The influence of the samurai in the culture that subsequently developed was strong. Kyoto's court culture was elegant, graceful, emotional, and effeminate; samurai culture was practical, ethical, vigorous, and masculine. Up to this time only the court and the nobles had been educated; they lived elegantly, absorbing and assimilating culture, and were completely isolated from the masses. The people were not touched by the life and culture of the aristocrats. Although the samurai were educated and had their roots among the aristocrats, they lived in the outlying districts, often in rural areas, and actually led a life much closer to that of the people. Because they had frequent contact with them, the samurai served to spread culture among them. This contact led to the rise of a people's culture, which blossomed during the subsequent Muromachi Period and flowered in the Edo (Tokugawa) Period, and to the birth of new sects of Buddhism for the people. Zen Buddhism, which so greatly influenced Japanese culture, was introduced in this era.

MUROMACHI PERIOD *1334–1573*

During this period Kyoto declined in power and many of the nobility, priests, and entertainers left the city, which contributed to the spread of culture among the people. Chinese influence was again strong, this time because of trade with China under the Yuan and Ming Dynasties. Noh masks, the Noh dance, the tea ceremony, gardens, the Shoin style of architecture, and the art of flower arrangement all developed in this period. The Shoin style refers to the house with a front entrance, mat-covered rooms, paper sliding doors, the tokonoma (alcove), etc., which is considered typically Japanese. The famous Kinkaku-ji (Golden Pavilion) and the Ginkaku-ji (Silver Pavilion) of Kyoto are products of this period, which is often compared to the Renaissance in Europe. It was during this period that European culture first entered Japan, as a result of trade with the Portuguese and Spaniards.

MOMOYAMA PERIOD *1573–1614*

In this period, Toyotomi Hideyoshi unified the country and laid the foundations of feudalism in Japan. Trade with the southeastern countries was conducted on a large scale; the spread of Christianity was tolerated; merchants and farmers became independent. Each new development contributed to Japanese culture. The influence of Buddhism on politics, economy, and culture dwindled. As a religion Buddhism was watered by collaboration with nature, Shinto, and the introduction of Confucian thought. The marks of feudalism—deep moats, massive stone walls, high castle towers—appeared all over the country. However, castle interiors were elegantly decorated, especially noteworthy were their gorgeous murals, for example, those at Osaka Castle. The tea ceremony, which became popu-

lar among feudal lords and rich merchants, culminated into an art under the influence of Sen Rikyu. The Noh plays and its music became popular among people of all levels of society. The samisen *(see page 72)* entered Japan from the Ryukyu Islands and led to the founding of *jyoruri* (ballad plays). European influence continued to filter in through Christian missionaries, and the traders brought in firearms, gunpowder, and printing and oil painting techniques. The Itsukushima Shrine built in the sixteenth century is a good example of the Japanese architecture of this period.

TOKUGAWA PERIOD *1615–1867*

During the first half of this period, which is also called the Edo Period, Kyoto, despite its political impotence, was still considered the cultural center of Japan. But the powerful merchant class in Osaka was fostering another cultural center, the center of a strongly developing people's culture. During the later half of this period, Edo (the present Tokyo) became both the capital of the nation and the center of Japanese culture. From the outset the Tokugawa Shoguns adopted the drastic policy of completely sealing in the whole country by closing the ports and oppressing Christianity. However, they also actively promoted the dissemination and assimilation of culture among all classes of people and brought about the flowering of culture. It was during this long era of domestic peace and almost complete isolation from the outside world that Edo and other urban areas expanded and developed. The rule of the Shoguns was rigid and society remained stratified, but it was during the Tokugawa Period that many of the customs and manners and the general patterns of living, which later became known abroad as typically Japanese, were established and spread throughout the country.

LIST OF ILLUSTRATIONS

木 *WOOD*

35
above: KENGAKU. Sekizo-ji, Kyoto
Offertory plaques. The temple is known for its divine power of extracting evil from the human body, thus the pincer-and-nail design on the plaques.
below: SHAKUSHI. Matsuo Shrine, Kyoto
Rice paddles used as votive objects.

36
TORII. Fushimi Inari Shrine, Kyoto
Miniature torii used as votive objects.

37
above left: KIGANFUDA. Amulets
above right: KENKA. Toji, Kyoto
Pails for floral offerings.
below left: KENSUIOKE. Yasaka Shrine, Kyoto
Pails for water offerings.
below right: KYOGI. Jyoan-ji, Kyoto
Sutra plaques offered to the dead.

38
KOSHI MADO. Ichiriki Teahouse, Gion, Kyoto
Latticed window with details of roof and outside wainscoting.

39
DEGOSHI MADO. Higashi Hongan-ji, Kyoto
Latticed window with details of roof and lower story.

40–41
SHOJIDO HIKITE. Mii Temple, Otsu
Pulls for opening and closing shoji.

42
above: MANEKI. Minami-za (Kabuki Theater), Kyoto
Placards advertising the names of actors.
center: KAMBAM. Shijo Hanamikoji, Kyoto
Signboard.
below: KAMBAM. Gion, Kyoto
Signboard.

43
KAMBAN. Takoyakushi, Kawaramachi-dori, Kyoto
Signboard advertising soy sauce.

44
IRIGUCHI. Hokoin, Yakushi-ji, Nara
Entry hall.

45
HASHIRA. East Corridor, Todai-ji, Nara
Detail of lacquered pillar and brace with painted stucco.

46
HARIYAMA. Detail of red-lacquered pincushion stand (see page 51)

47
IKO (formerly called IKA or KAKEYA). Black-lacquered clothes rack

48–49
IKO. Black-lacquered clothes rack
The torii design is comparatively new.

50
ITO GURUMA. Reel for winding silk

51
left: HARIYAMA. Pincushion stand
above right: HI. Four types of shuttles
below right: ITOMAKI. Square spools of thread

52–53
KUSHI. Combs made of boxwood
Boxwood is considered ideal for combs and has been used since the Heian Period.

54
left: KYOSOKU. Armrest
right: KAGAMI. Lacquered mirror (in case) and stand
The mirror was introduced from China early in the eighth century and did not change in form until the Tokugawa Period, when a mirror with handle and stand was introduced.

55
above: SUMIBI. Charcoal in pit of brazier, as seen from above
below: NAGAHIBACHI. Rectangular brazier with drawers
Normally the measurements are 2' × 1'2" × 1'1". The drawers are for miscellaneous items. This type of brazier became popular during the Tokugawa Period.

56–57
FUMIDAI. Footstool
The hollow interior of these two-step stools is used for storage.

58–59

SOROBAN. Abaci

The abacus was introduced from China into Japan toward the end of the Muromachi Period when trade with China developed.

60

GO ISHI and GO BAN. Sets of black and white Go pieces and Go board

Go is a Japanese game which, according to one legend, was introduced to China from India and thence to Japan. Another story holds that Go originated in China 3,000 years ago.

61

SHOGI KOMA and SHOGI BAN. Shogi marker and Shogi board

Shogi is the Japanese form of chess. It is said to have originated in India, but was introduced to Japan from China. In Japan the game has changed considerably. The biggest difference is that in shogi, captured pieces can be used by the captor.

62

GETA. Men's clogs

Geta were developed during the Tokugawa Period. The material for geta must be light and strong; paulownia wood and Japanese cedar are considered the best materials.

63

GETA. Women's clogs

64

GETA. Lacquered clogs for women, men, and children

65

SUMITSUBO. Carpenter's marker, used to make an inked line for sawing

The sumitsubo is said to have been in use since the Nara Period. The string is played out from the reel and passes over an inked pad. The inked string is then secured to the plank of wood by a small gimlet to insure a straight line. However, a curved line can also be drawn.

66

DARUMA. Toy in the shape of Daruma, with a top built into the head

A popular toy in the Tohoku District.

67

KOKESHI. A type of doll that originated in the Tohoku District

It became popular during the Tokugawa Period.

68–69

NOH MEN. Noh masks

top row: DEIGAN. A woman's soul or death mask, very righteous and refined. SHIKAMI. A demon in wrath. MIKAZUKI. Spirit of an inhuman man. CHUJO. A young man of the nobility. KOUSHINOJO. An old man (personification of Kami or God). SHOJO. A cheerful elf.

center row: SHUNKAN. A man full of sadness but withholding it. KO-OMOTE. A young, pure woman of the nobility. YAMAUBA. An old hag of the mountains, very fierce. HANNYA. A revengeful ghost, representing woman's tenaciousness. YAMAUBA. An old woman.

bottom row: MASUKAMI. Expresses tenacity. OKINA. An aged man, representing long life and prosperity. FUKAI. A middle-aged woman who has undergone the trials and tribulations of life. KAWAZU. Man's sadness. KASSHIKI. A lad who serves in the Zen temple. OOBESHIMI. An exaggerated expression of egoism and arrogance.

The Noh is a Japanese lyrical drama in which players wear masks. Each mask has a name and each represents symbolically the emotions of the characters in the drama, such as joy, sorrow, anger, happiness, as well as youth, age, beauty, etc.

70–71

KASHIRA. Puppet heads for the Bunraku Theater, the representative puppet show of Japan

top row: DAIDANSHICHI. A samurai at war. WAKA-OTOKO. A young man of the world.

center row: OTE GOZEN. A middle-aged woman. BUNSHICHI. A dashing young man. OSOME. A young girl. KEIJO. A courtesan. CHUJO HIME. A princess. KOYAKU. A child actor

bottom row: DANSHICHI. A samurai. BUNSHICHI. A young lover. BUNSHICHI. A young lover. DANSHICHI. A samurai. AKUBABA. A vicious old hag.

Each puppet, which is made up of head, trunk, and limbs, is manipulated by three men. (Female puppets do not have legs since the kimono hides the lower part of the body.) The puppets are so exquisitely made that the eyes, mouth, and even the eyebrows move, as well as the joints of the hands and feet.

72

left and center: SHAMISEN. A three-stringed lute

The samisen was introduced to Japan around 1562 from Ryukyu Islands and evolved to its present form during the Tokugawa Period. Various types of samisen are used to accompany Japanese singing.
right: KENDAI. Rostrum
Used by singers.

73

BACHI. Plectrum (ivory) for the samisen
Ivory is the most commonly used material for the plectrum. Buffalo bone, boxwood, and oak are also used.

74

TSUZUMI. A shoulder drum
A long drum placed on the right shoulder. It is beaten with the left hand while the strings are controlled by the fingers of the right hand to achieve different tones. Originally from China, it is popularly used to accompany the Noh drama.

75

TAIKO. Large drum played in a sitting position
The skin of the drum is either nailed or pasted to the rim.

76–77

KOTO (details). A harp or zither-like instrument of thirteen strings played in a sitting position
The koto is a musical instrument indigenous to Japan. In prehistoric days it had five strings; by the eighth century, six strings; and today it has thirteen strings. The frame is usually made of paulownia wood and is about six feet long. The supports for the strings are made of ivory. Ivory "finger nails" are slipped on to the inside tip of three fingers of the right hand, the thumb and the first two fingers, which are then used to plunk down on the strings.

78–79

BIWA. A five-stringed lutelike instrument (plectrum at far right)
A five-stringed instrument that came from China during the Nara Period. During the Momoyama Period the Satsuma style biwa (3' long with four strings) was popular among the samurai. In the nineteenth century the Chikuzen style biwa (2'3" with four or five strings) was originated. The plectrum is made of ginkgo wood.

80

MASU. Measuring boxes for solids, such as rice (above), and for liquids, such as sake (below)
These contain standard measurements which were first established in 1586 by the ruler Toyotomi Hideyoshi.

81

above: MESHI BITSU. Container for cooked rice
below: SHAMOJI. Rice paddles used to transfer cooked rice
Shrines began to issue shamoji as amulets during the Tokugawa Period.

82–83

above: SHUKI. A nest of three lacquered sake cups and a lacquered sake pitcher
center: SHIRU WAN. Lacquered soup bowls, seen from the side and above
The shuki and soup bowls are used on festive occasions.
below: MANAITA. Chopping or cutting board
far right: HASHI. Chopsticks in paper wrapper
This type is used on festive occasions.

84

above right: HASHI. Paired chopsticks with box and cover
above left: HASHI. Chopsticks on rests
Bamboo, wood, and ivory are used to make hashi. Some are of natural wood, some are lacquered.
below: BON. Tray
Trays are of all shapes and design, most are lacquered.

85

above: YOJI. Willow and spicebush toothpicks and container
Toothpicks are usually of willow, but in recent times spicebush toothpicks have become popular.
below: BON. Lacquered tray

86–87

left and right: JUBAKO. Nests of lacquered boxes for carrying food
Jubako became increasingly popular from the end of the Muromachi Period to the end of the Tokugawa Period. Later, jubako with handles were introduced for outings. To this day, they are used during the New Year holidays or on Girls' Festival Day (March 3). The boxes are lacquered both on the outside and inside, usually with gold designs.

88

above: TSUNODARU. Sake keg for sake offerings to Shinto deities (kami)
Most are lacquered in red and take their names from the handles in the shape of horns, tsuno.
below: SHAKU. Ladles used for tea ceremony, generally of wood or bamboo

89

WAN. Lacquered soup bowl with pine design

90

HIGASHI. Confections
Higashi are dry sweets first made in the Heian Period from dried and granulated peels of pine nuts, acorns, pomagranate, and Chinese dates, which have been steamed. Since the Muromachi Period, they have been made of rice flour and sugar. These sweets are served mainly with tea at ceremonial gatherings.

91

KIGATA. Wooden forms used for making higashi

92

SUZURI BAKO. Black lacquer writing box
Suzuri bako, or writing box, takes its name from suzuri, the ink stone. Suzuri bako contains the ink stone, the ink bar, a small metal water container, paper cutter, and brushes. Ink stone and brush writing were adopted some time between 400–300 B.C.

93

above: JUZU. Buddhist rosaries
The beads are counted as the sutra are chanted. The size of the beads differs according to the Buddhist sect. The rosaries are made of nuts, crystal, coral, aromatic woods, and linden. Rosaries have 1,080, 180, 54, or 27 beads, although some have 36 or 18 beads. Today they are used as prayer beads.
below: MOKUGYO. Drum or wooden gong, on cushion, used in Buddhist services
Drummed by priests as they chant the sutra. In the early days the wood was carved in the shape of a hollow fish; later the shape was changed to that of a dragon with two heads. It originated in China as a wooden gong for calling people together.

94

IHAI. Buddhist mortuary tablet in memory of the dead
The name of the deceased is carved on the tablet and it is placed in the household Buddhist shrine.

紙 *PAPER*

96
GOHEI. Yasaka Shrine, Kyoto
A sacred staff or wand deocrated with paper cuttings used in Shinto shrines and ceremonies for purposes of purification.

97
SEMBA ZURU. Azumamaru Shrine, Fushimi, Kyoto
Thousand cranes. The cranes are of folded paper, in a manner said to have originated during the Heian Period, and are strung together. Today semba zuru are offered at shrines in supplication. The folding of cranes is also a pastime of the children, known as origami.

98
above: GOHEI. Azumamaru Shrine, Fushimi, Kyoto
Paper cuttings made and hung to insure purification, with detail of bell ropes.
below: NAFUDA. Mimuro Temple, Uji
Name cards of suppliants offered at shrines.

99
MIKUJI. Kiyosu-kojin Shrine, Takarazuka, Hyogo Prefecture
Paper fortunes obtained at shrines, secured to the latticework or offertory boxes and left behind by the believers.

100
above: SHUGO FUDA. Sumiya, Shimabara, Kyoto
Paper amulets left behind (next to painted mask) by worshipers for protection and good luck and to exorcise malignant diseases.

below: KAMIBATA. Inari Shrine, Kyoto
Small paper banners, about 8" long, fastened to sticks and left along the road to the shrine for protection and good luck.

101
above: DARUMA. Daruma Temple, Kyoto
Daruma dolls, souvenirs of the Temple. Daruma was the great Buddhist teacher who is said to have meditated for ten years with his legs crossed, with the result that his arms and legs disappeared and his body became a lump shaped much as these dolls. The dolls are painted bright red, the color of Daruma's robe. Since the beginning of the nineteenth century the doll has been a symbol of good luck for people engaged in sericulture, farming, and fishing.
below: KIGAN FUDA. Kitano Shrine, Kyoto
Prayer placards used as votives, illustrated with birds and the name of the person seeking good luck and prosperity in business.

102–105
SHOJI. Sumiya, Shimabara, Kyoto
Rice-paper sliding doors, designed during the Tokugawa Period for use in private homes. The shoji shown on these pages were designated as Important Cultural Property in 1952.

106–107
SHOJI. Hokke-ji, Nara
These shoji have decorated rice-paper inserts.

108
SHOJIDO. Daruma Temple, Kyoto
Paper sliding doors fitted with wood and decorated with image of Daruma.

109
SHOJIDO. Kiyomizu Temple, Kyoto
Double sliding doors.

110
left: ANDON. Kyo Horiya (doll shop), Gion, Kyoto
Rice-paper lamp with name. In the middle of the Muromachi Period the andon was held in the hand and used to light the way when walking at night. Later it became popular to use them for lighting houses.
right: ANDON. Sumiya, Shimabara, Kyoto
Rice-paper lamp, eighteenth century.

111
ANDON. Karafune, Gion, Kyoto
Rice-paper lamp with protective mesh and openwork boat design.

112
MIYAMAIRI FUDA. Yasaka Shrine, Kyoto
Paper charms left behind by worshipers on pilgrimage, intended to insure good fortune. In Japan when baby boys are 33 days old and girls are 30 days old, they are taken to visit a shrine to pray for good fortune and protection, and such charms are offered to the deities.

113
SEMBA ZURU. Kiyosu-kojin, Takarazuka
Paper cranes and paper fortune.

114–115
SENSU. Miyawaki Sensu, Rokkakutomikoji, Kyoto
Paper fans on display.

116
above: MAIOGI. Paper dancing fan, bamboo with gold decorations
This type of fan dates from the early part of the Heian Period. Today such fans are used with formal attire for dancing in the Noh drama.
below: ORIGAMI. The art of paper folding, or the folded paper objects such as these: Hakama (man's skirt), Yakko (a footman), and Kabuto (a helmet).

117
NOSHI and MIZUHIKI. Formal decorations used on gifts, on the occasion of exchanging betrothal gifts, as well as when presenting gifts
The noshi, a symbolic bundle of dried abalone folded in paper, is usually placed at the upper right-hand corner of a gift package, and the mizuhiki (red and white or silver and gold strings used for tying presents) is tied in various ways around the mid-section. Combinations of red and white or silver and gold mizuhiki are used for presents on felicitous or auspicious occasions, and black and white or yellow and white mizuhiki when giving a gift on sad or unfortunate occasions, such as funerals, wakes, etc.

118
HANAFUDA. Japanese playing cards
These cards became popular during the Tokugawa Period. A set consists of 48 cards, each showing some flower, bird, moon, or scene indicating one of the four seasons.

119
ORIGAMI. Paper foldings representing: a boat; the sambo (small tray on stand used for sacred offerings); a paper balloon; a crane

120
OGI. Paper folding fans with bamboo fittings

121
UCHIWA. Fan with handle, made of paper and bamboo
The uchiwa, introduced from China, became popular during the Tokugawa Period. It is used as a common household item.

122–123
EMA. Takayama, Gifu Prefecture
A votive picture of a horse donated to the shrine by the suppliant. At first the ema was used to pray for the safety of horses and cattle, but it came to be used to pray for the safety of the family and for prosperity.

124
GOFU. Kannon-ji, Abiko, Osaka
Paper amulets.

125
HAMAYA. Fushimi Inari Shrine, Kyoto
Sacred arrow (center) to exorcise evil, and decorated paper wands.

126–127
CHOCHIN. Paper lanterns with handles
Such lanterns have been in use since the middle of the Muromachi Period to light the way when walking at night. Below right: shade lowered for lighting.

128–129
JANOME GASA. Paper umbrellas
The umbrella is said to have originated during the Tokugawa Period. Janome gasa means, literally, an umbrella with a dragon's eye design. It is made of oiled paper and bamboo.

130–131
TAKO. Kites, from northern Japan
The kite on page 130 is called tsugaru and is from Aomori Prefecture; the kite on page 131 is rokkaku (literally, hexagon) from Niigata Prefecture.

132
TAKO. Kites, from central Japan
Tomoe (left) and tongari (right), both from Yokosuka. The origin of Japanese kites is unknown.

133
SAGEGAMI. Paper cutouts used to decorate the house entrance and the household Buddhist altar during the New Year season
This practice is popular in Sado, Niigata Prefecture. Sagegami means, literally, hanging paper.

134
left: MAKIGAMI. Paper roll for writing letters
right: JYO. Folded paper book with brocade cover
A quire of paper or folded paper strips made by pasting together folded sheets of paper 6″ × 6½″, often bound into booklets that open like a screen.

135
above: SHIKISHI. Square pieces of thick heavy paper, usually colored or patterned, used for writing or painting
below: TANZAKU. Long strips of thick heavy paper used for writing poetry

136–137
JORURI BON. Script and score for joruri dramatic ballad sung to the accompaniment of the samisen.
This type of singing originated during the Muromachi Period. Today the Bunraku Puppet Shows are acted to the accompaniment of joruri.

138
KIYOMOTO HON. Cover of kiyomoto script book
Kiyomoto is another type of ballad drama, also sung to the accompaniment of the samisen. Kiyomoto became popular during the Tokugawa Period.

139
TOKIWAZU HON. Script for another type of ballad singing accompanied by the samisen
This type of ballad singing is closely connected with the Kabuki Theater.

140
OMIKUJI. Miyake Hachiman Shrine, Kyoto
Paper fortune left fastened to the facing of a shrine door.

土 CLAY

Stratified clay and stone wall.
below: DOBEI. Pontocho, Kyoto
Small panel for a wall, baked clay with fenestra design of birds.

156–157

above: MIKE and MIKI. Kitano Tenman Shrine, Kyoto
Sacred clay utensils used in shrines when offering food and drink to Shinto deities.
below left: KUMOGATA KAWARAKE. Kitano Tenman Shrine, Kyoto
Clay cloud-design cups for drinking sacred sake at Shinto sanctuaries.
below right: MIKI. Kitano Tenman Shrine, Kyoto
Clay sake bottles with paper squills, after offering.

158

top right: NATSUME. Glazed container for powdered ceremonial tea
central group: MATCHA CHAWAN. Bowls for matcha (powdered tea), used for ceremonial tea drinking
The cult of drinking tea was introduced to Japan from China during the Kamakura Period and was refined by the famous contemporary tea master, Sen Rikyu, into the ritual of the tea ceremony. Tea bowls are appreciated more for their shape than for designs on them.

159

SHUKI. Set of sake cups and bottles

160

above left: SAKAZUKI. Sake cup
below left and above right: CHOSHI. Sake bottles
The name choshi was adopted in the Meiji Period.
below right: HYOTAN. Gourd flask

161

above: YUNOMI CHAWAN. Ordinary teacups used for drinking tea
center: YAKUMI IRE. Condiment containers
bottom: FUTATSUKI YUNOMI CHAWAN. Teacups with covers

162–163

left and bottom right: MESHI CHAWAN. Rice bowls, seen from the side and from above
above and center right: DOBIN. Teapots, seen from the side and from above

164–165

SARA. Plates. KOBACHI. Small bowls. TOKKURI. Small bottles
Round and rectangular bowls, plates, and small bottles for holding sake, soy sauce, etc.

166

KATAKUCHI. Beaked bowl of glazed clay for pouring soy sauce or sake

167

SURIBACHI and SURIKOGI. Suribachi, clay mortar used for grinding or crushing seasame and other foods; surikogi, the wooden pestle used with the suribachi
Believed to have been in use in the Heian Period.

168

HIBACHI. From Tottori Prefecture
Clay brazier. A very large bowl filled with ash upon which charcoal is burned to warm the room.

169

HIBACHI. Hokke-ji, Nara
Glazed clay brazier made during the Nara Period, from Hokke-ji, Nara. The name hibachi is believed to have originated during the Muromachi Period.

170

KAMADO. A cooking stove
Just as other primitive peoples believed in gods of the hearth, the Japanese believed in a Shinto deity of the Kamado, called Hettsui or Kudo, who protected the family. The site of the Kamado, therefore, was considered a sacred place, the spiritual center of family or society, and a place to worship one's ancestors.

木

WOOD

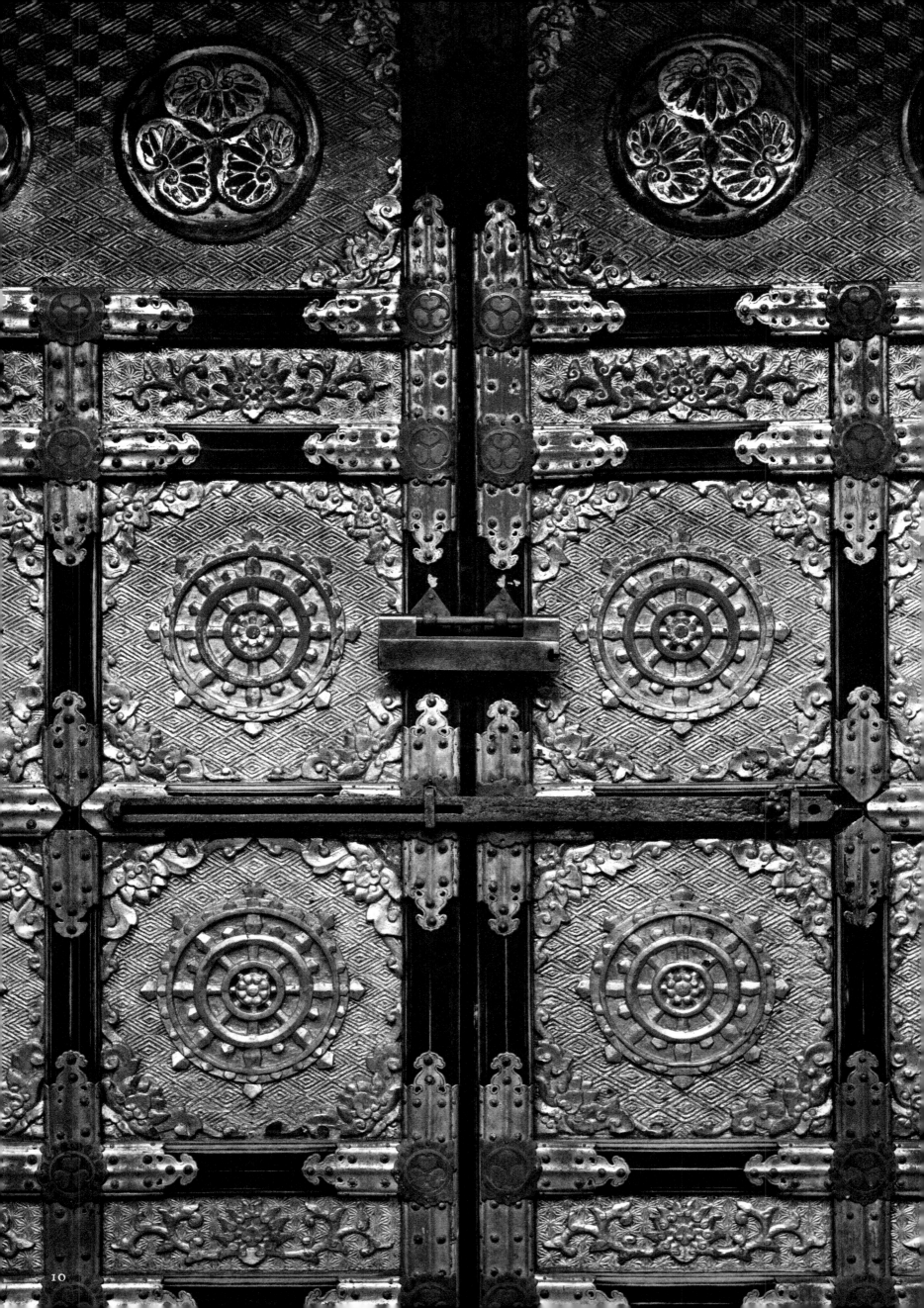

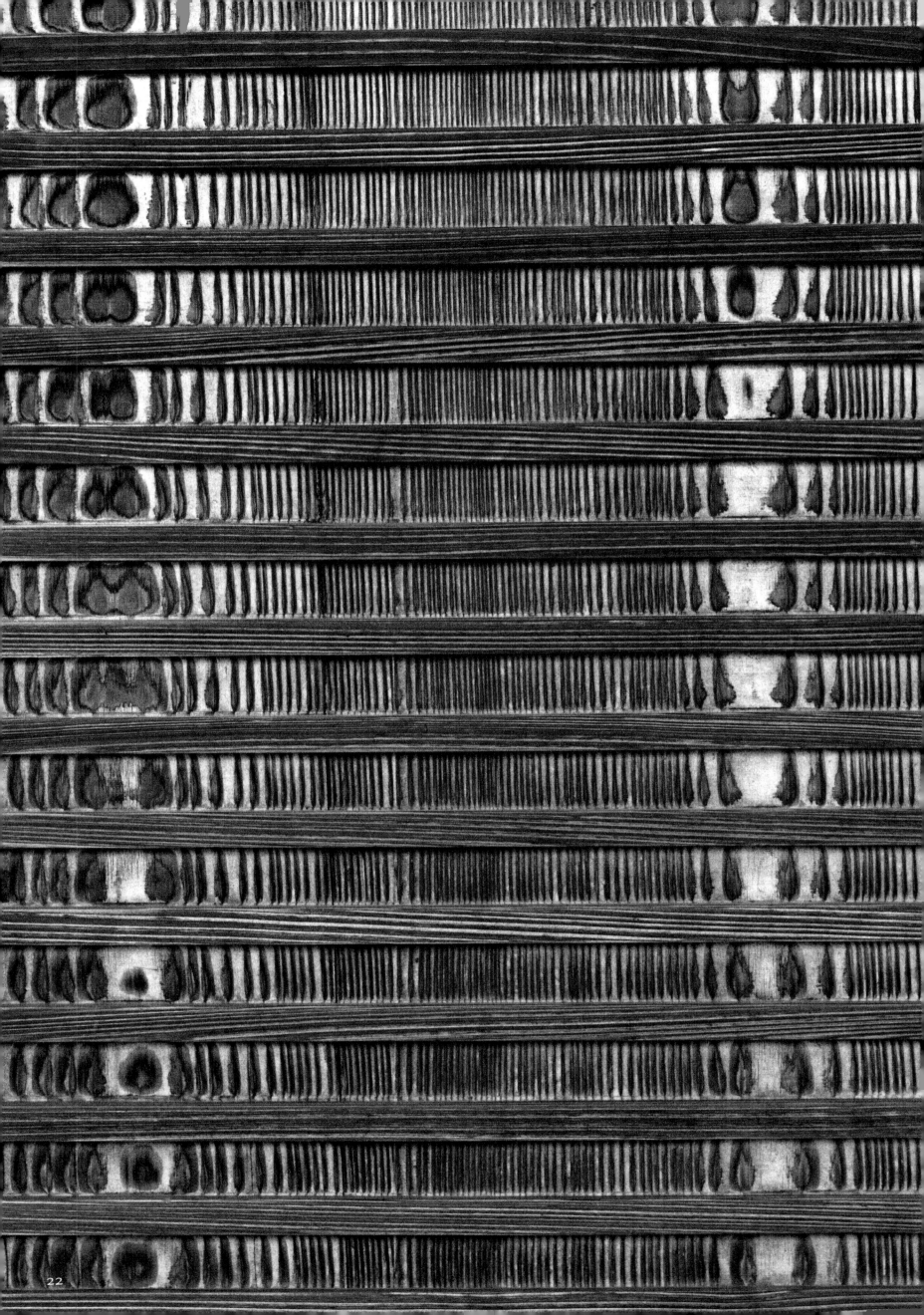

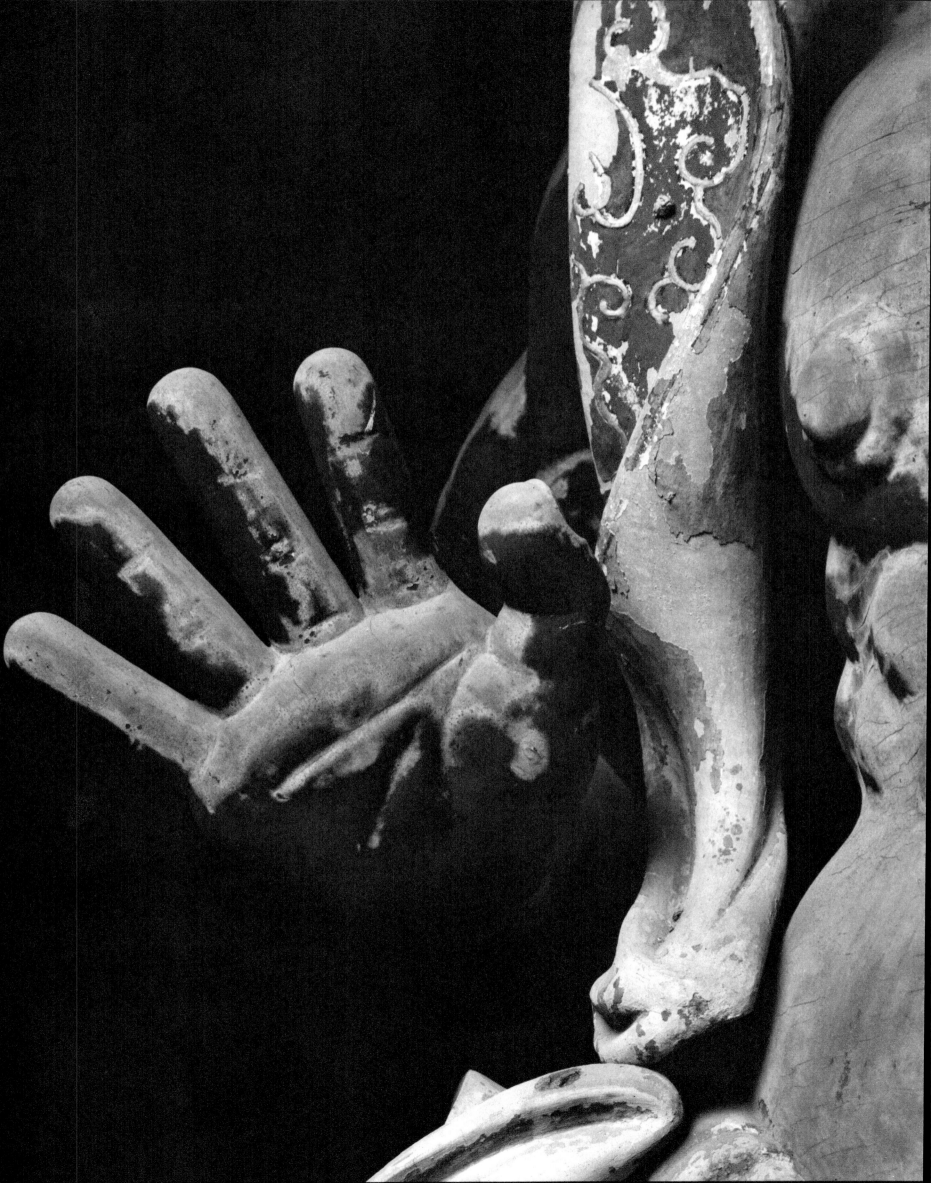

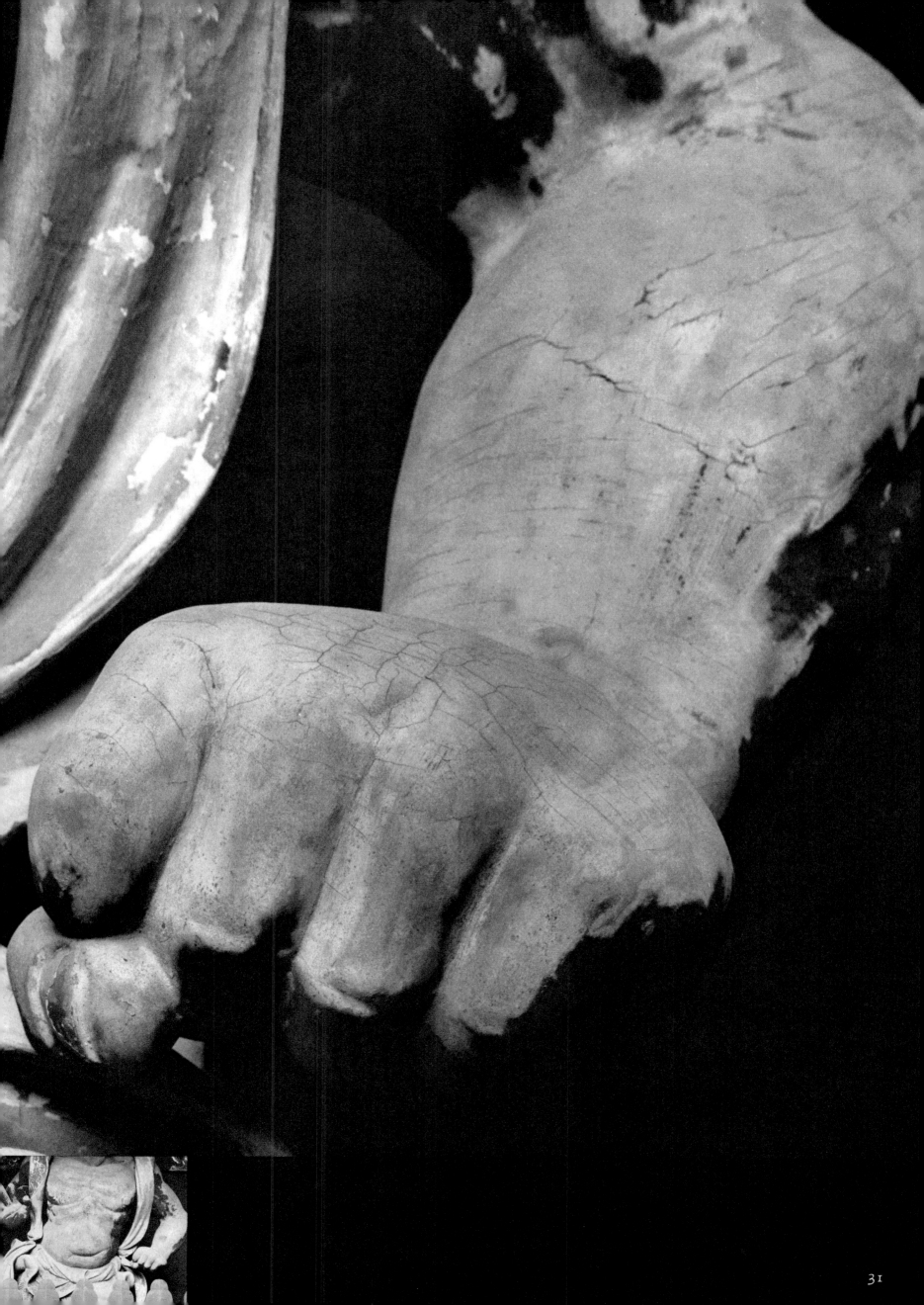

奉納

第拾番　山城國　御室堂

嘉永七年

かゝる世にうまれあふみの

われなれやねがふもおなじ

みのりなりけり

願主　大阪堂嶋

　大堀氏

釋清岸童女

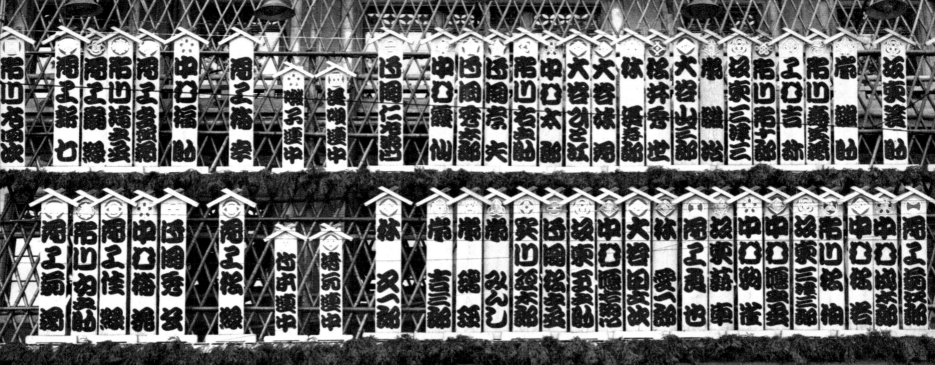

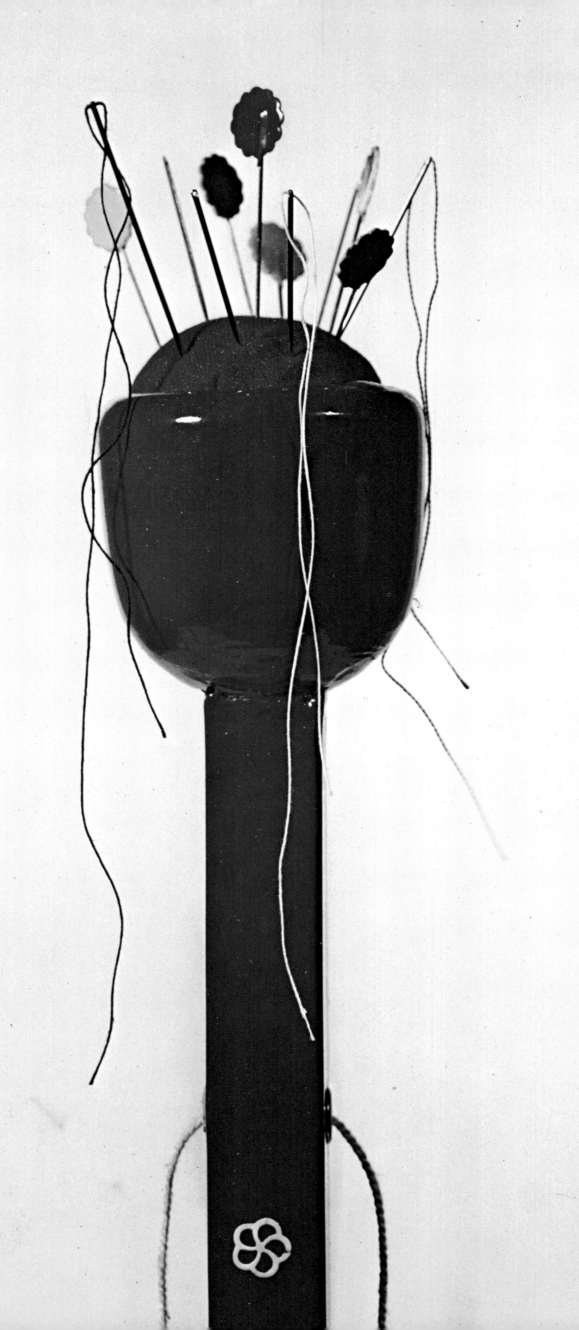

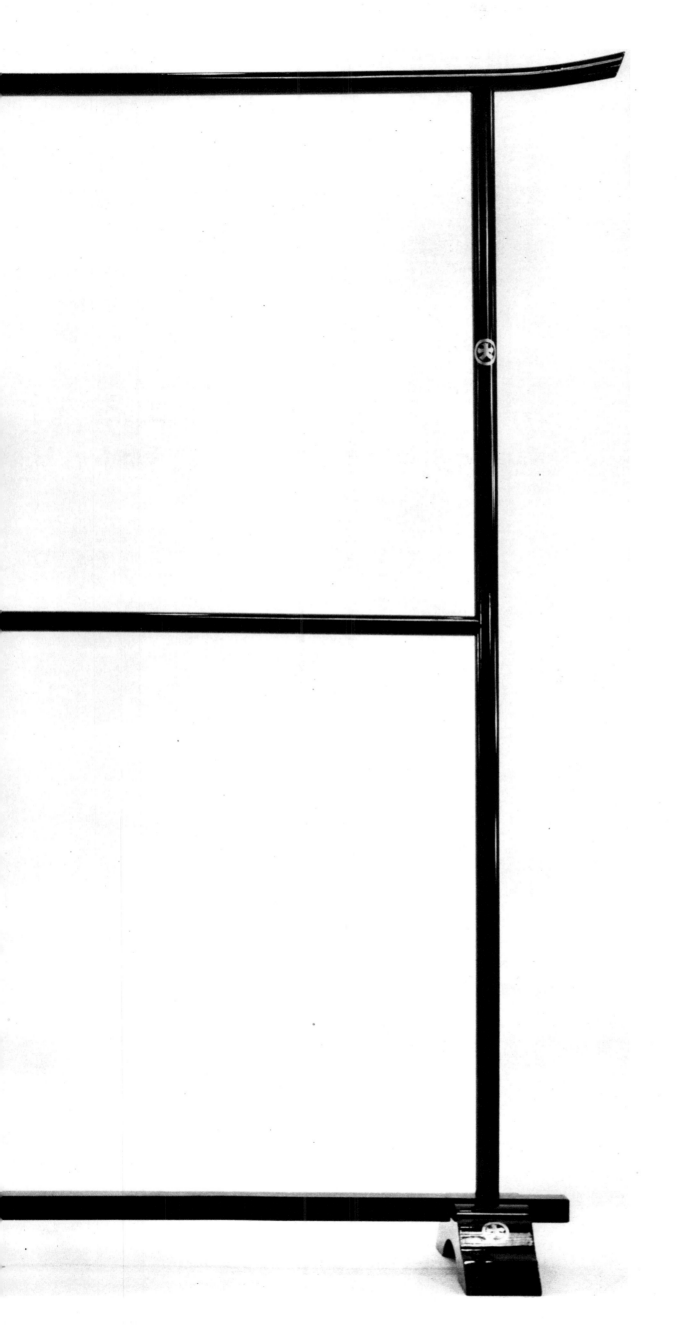

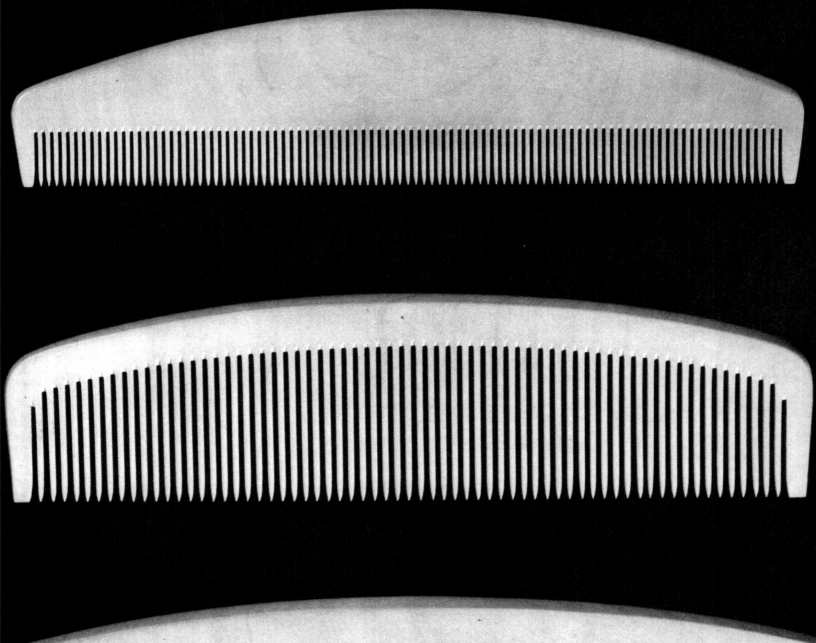

53

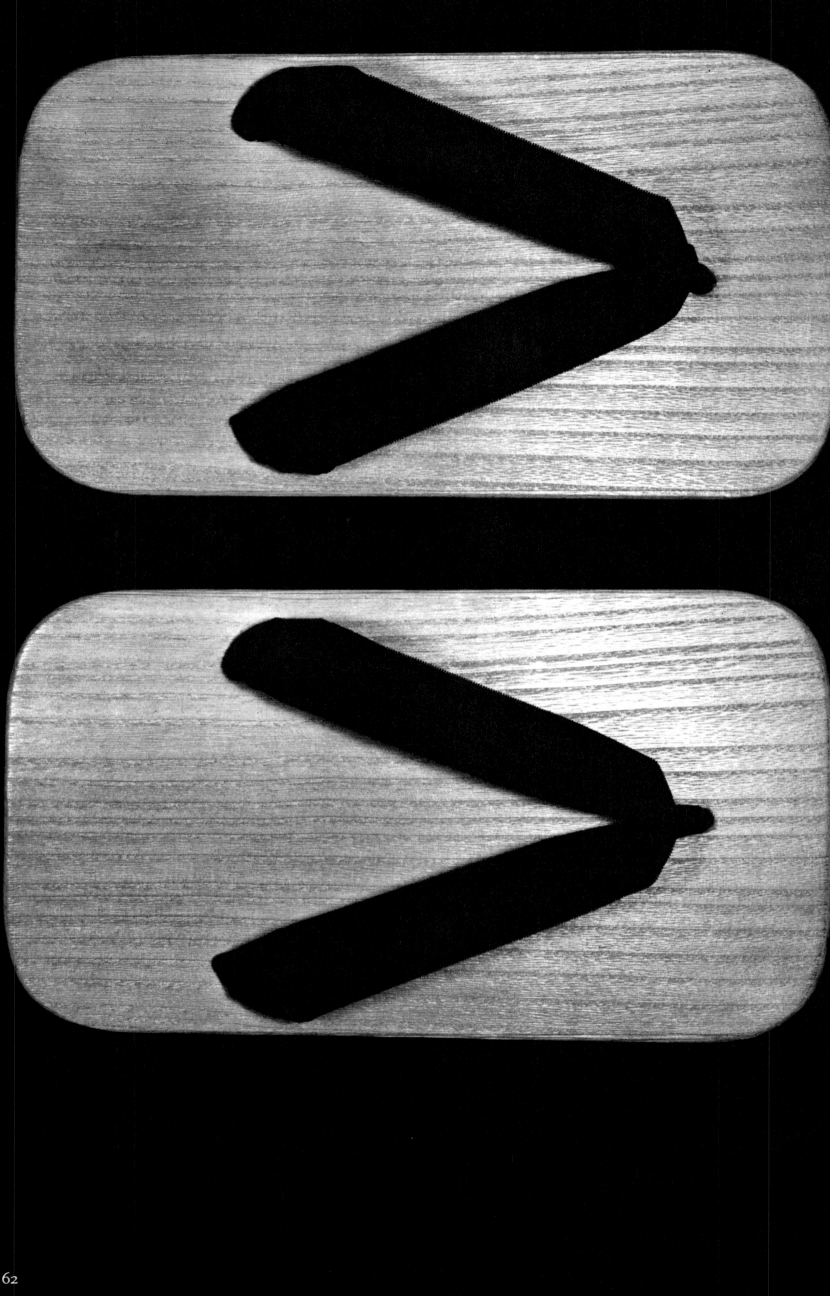

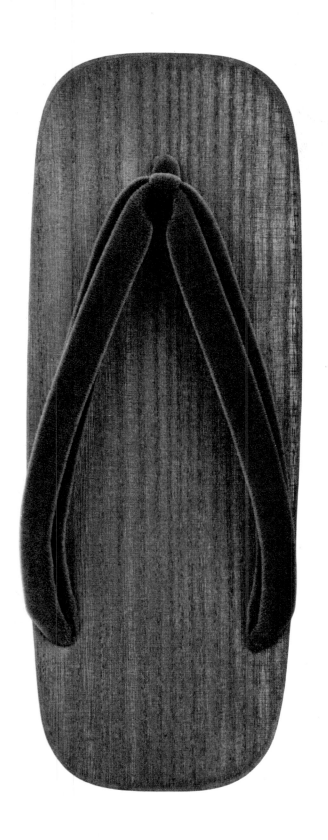
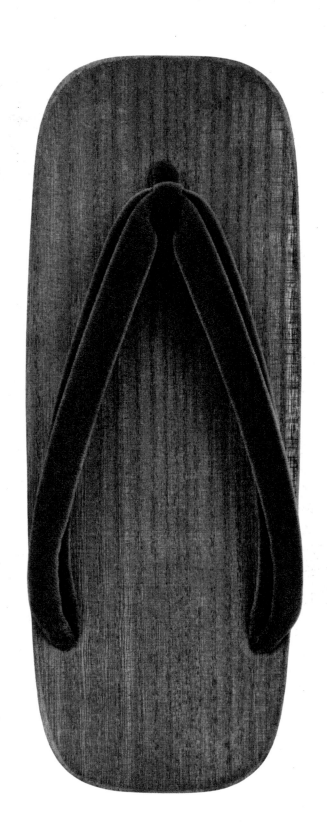

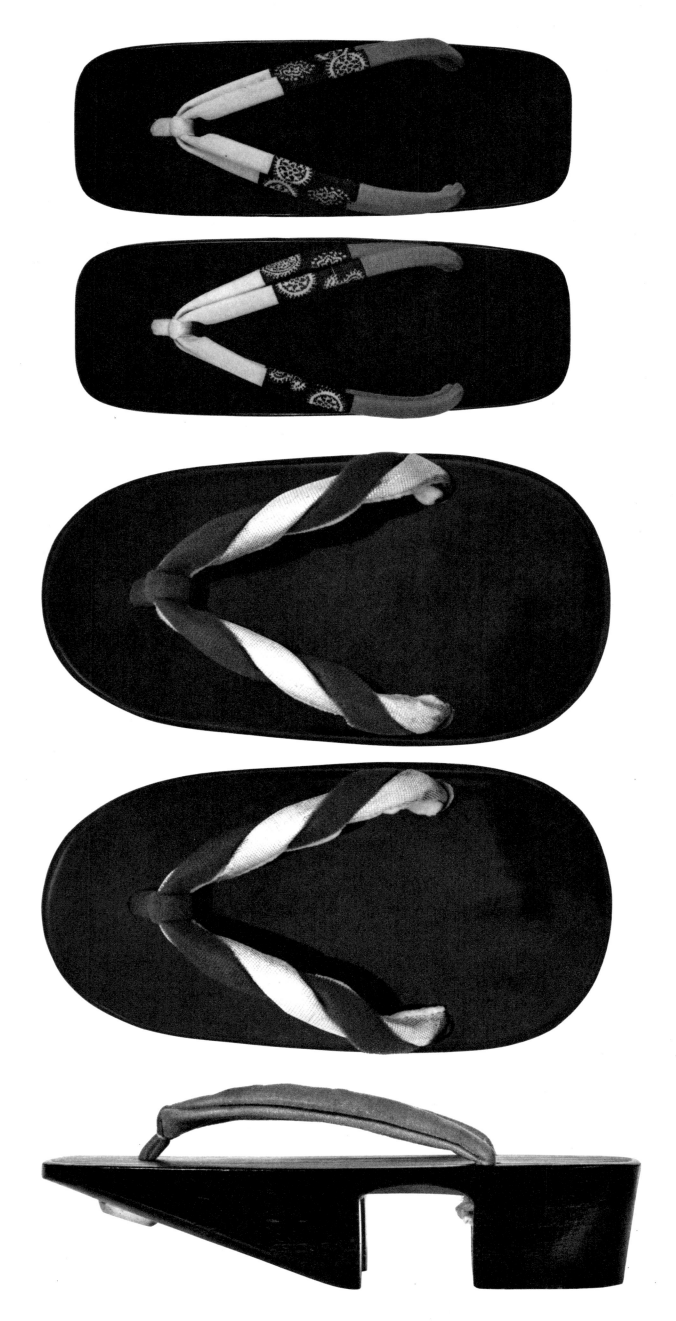

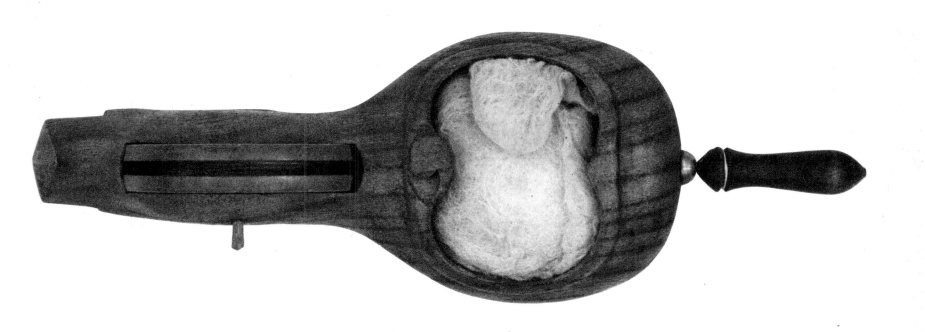

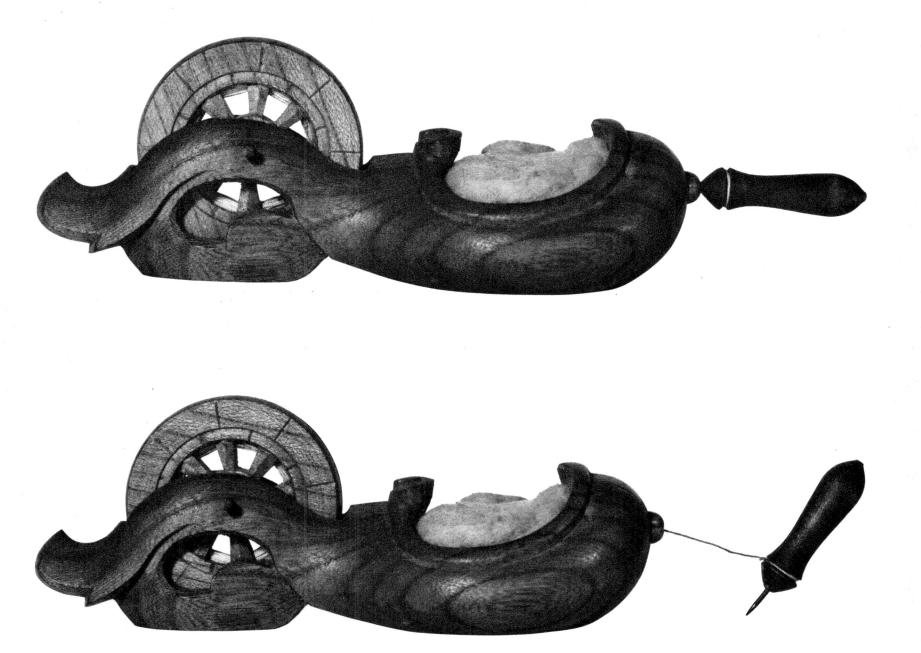

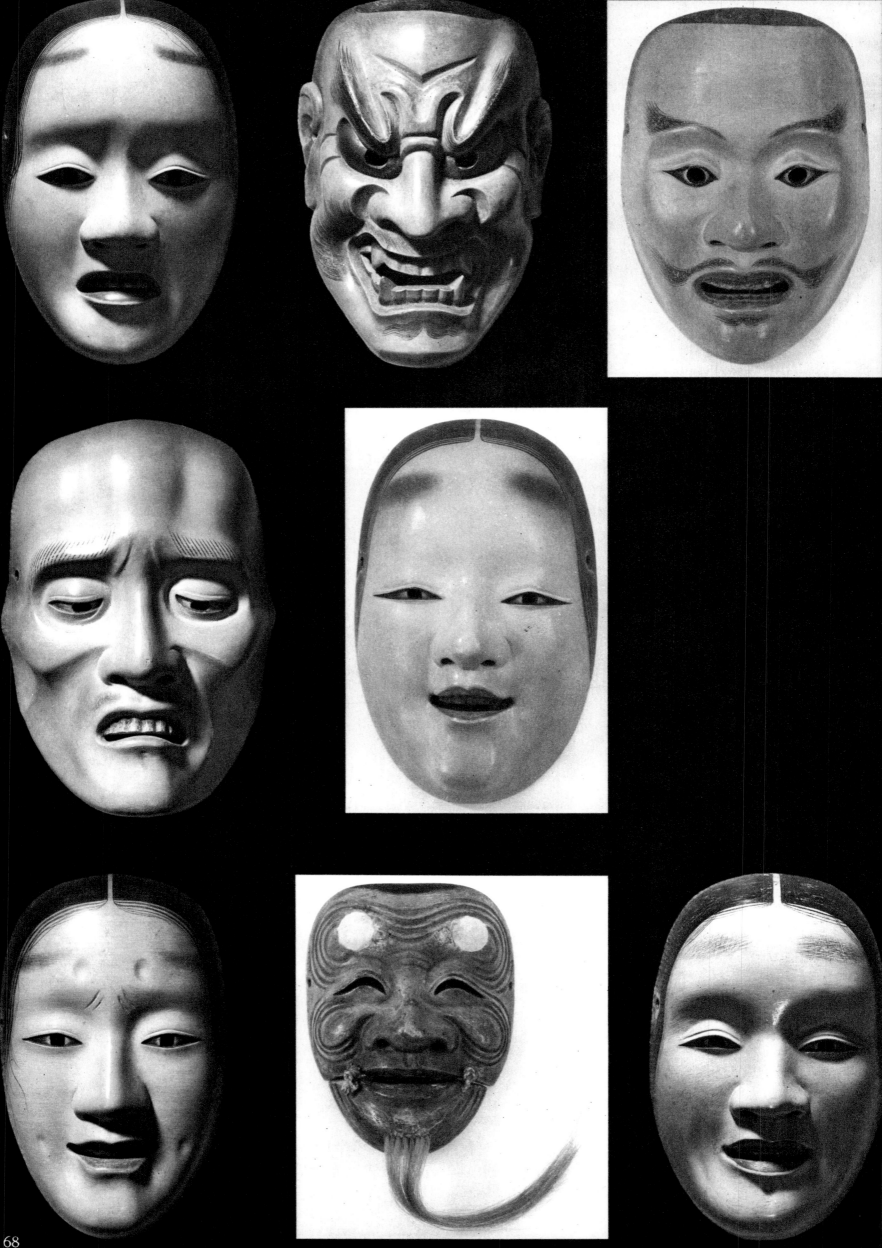

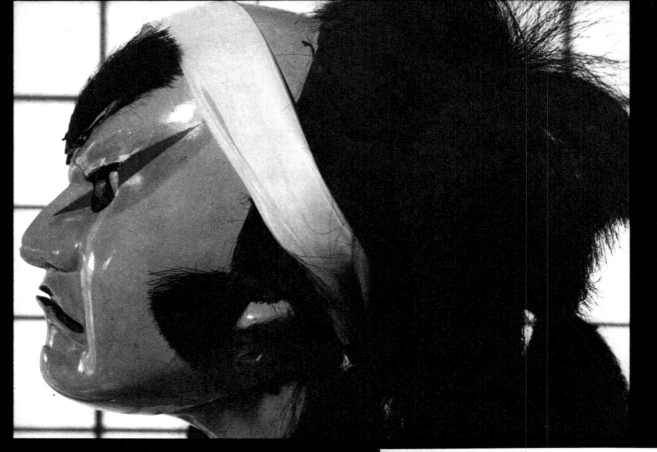

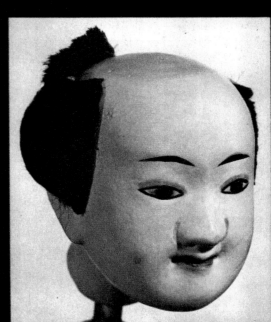

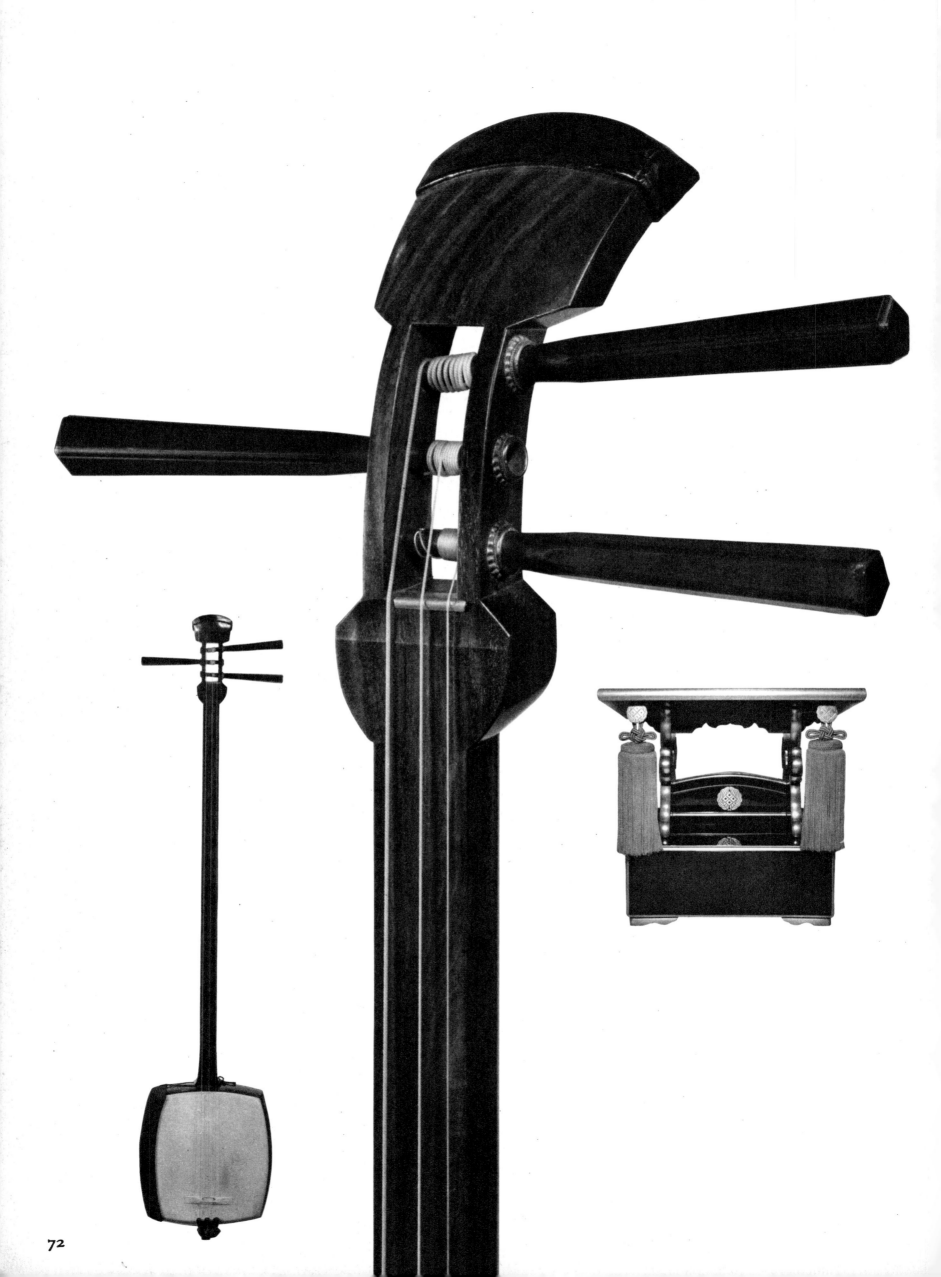

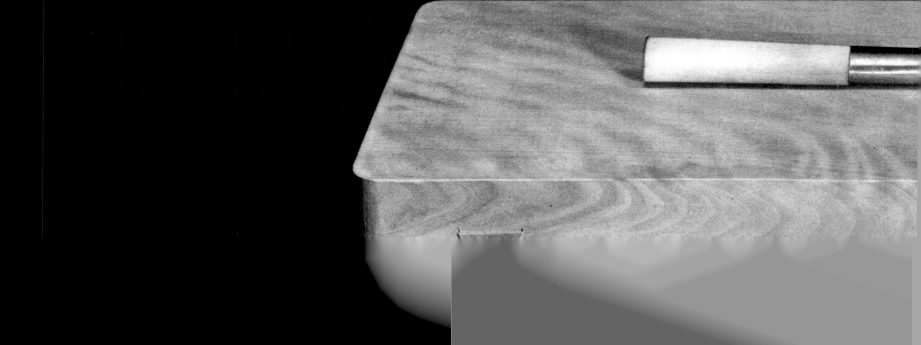

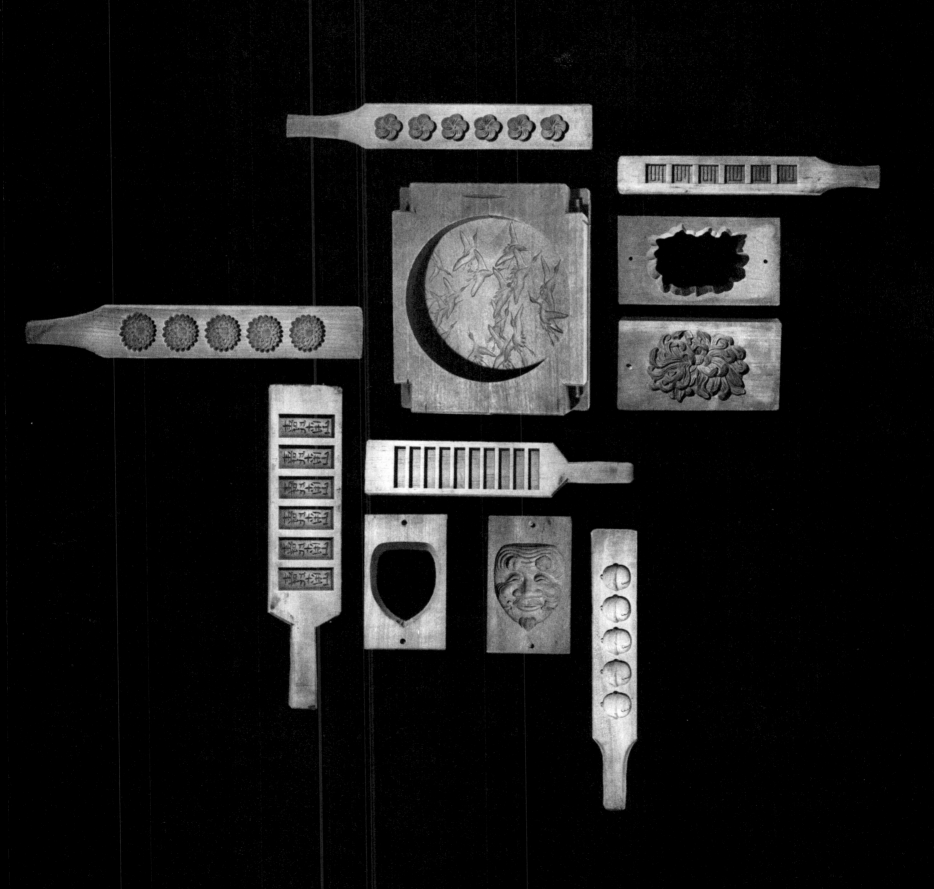

紙

PAPER

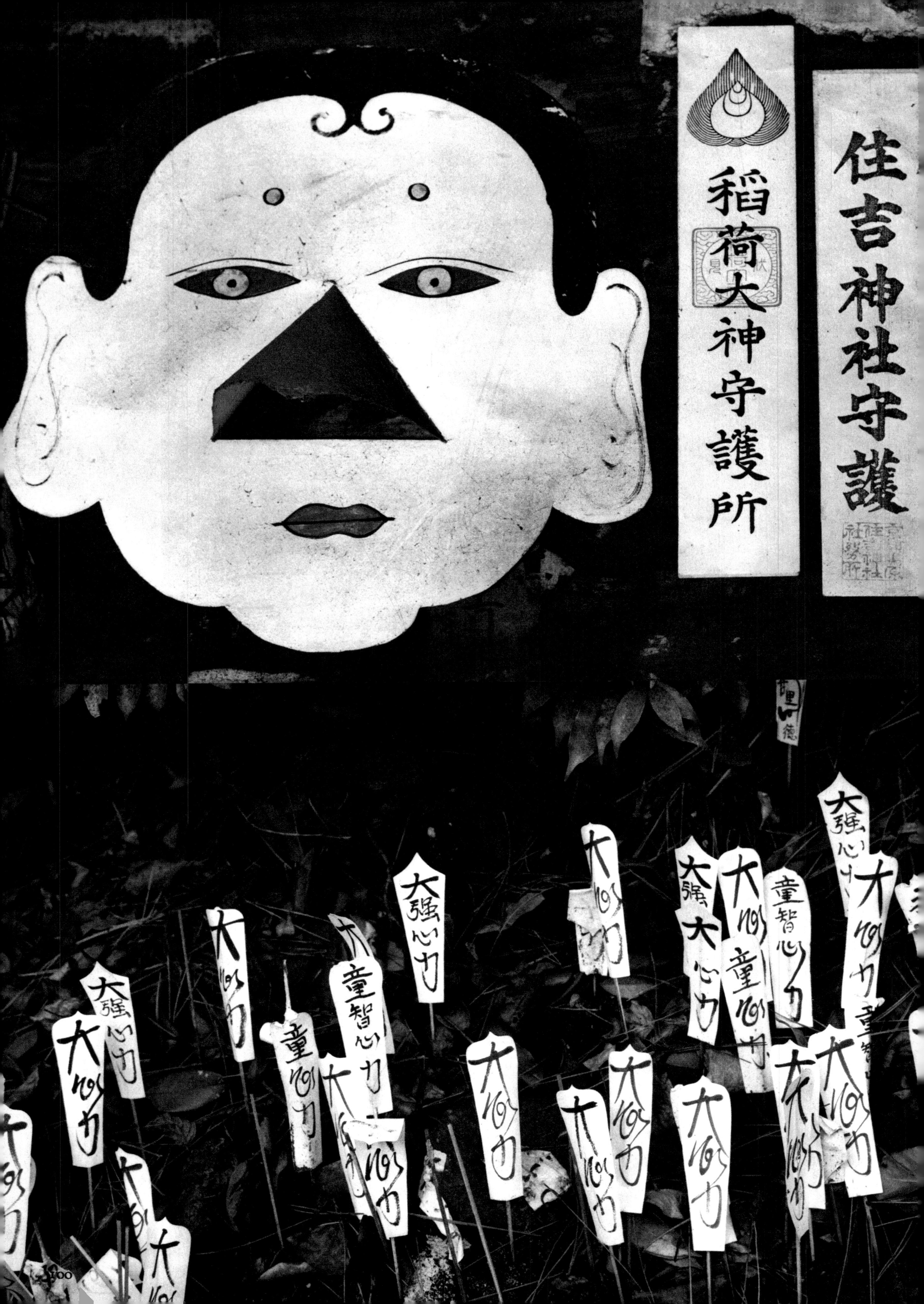
稲荷大神守護所
住吉神社守護

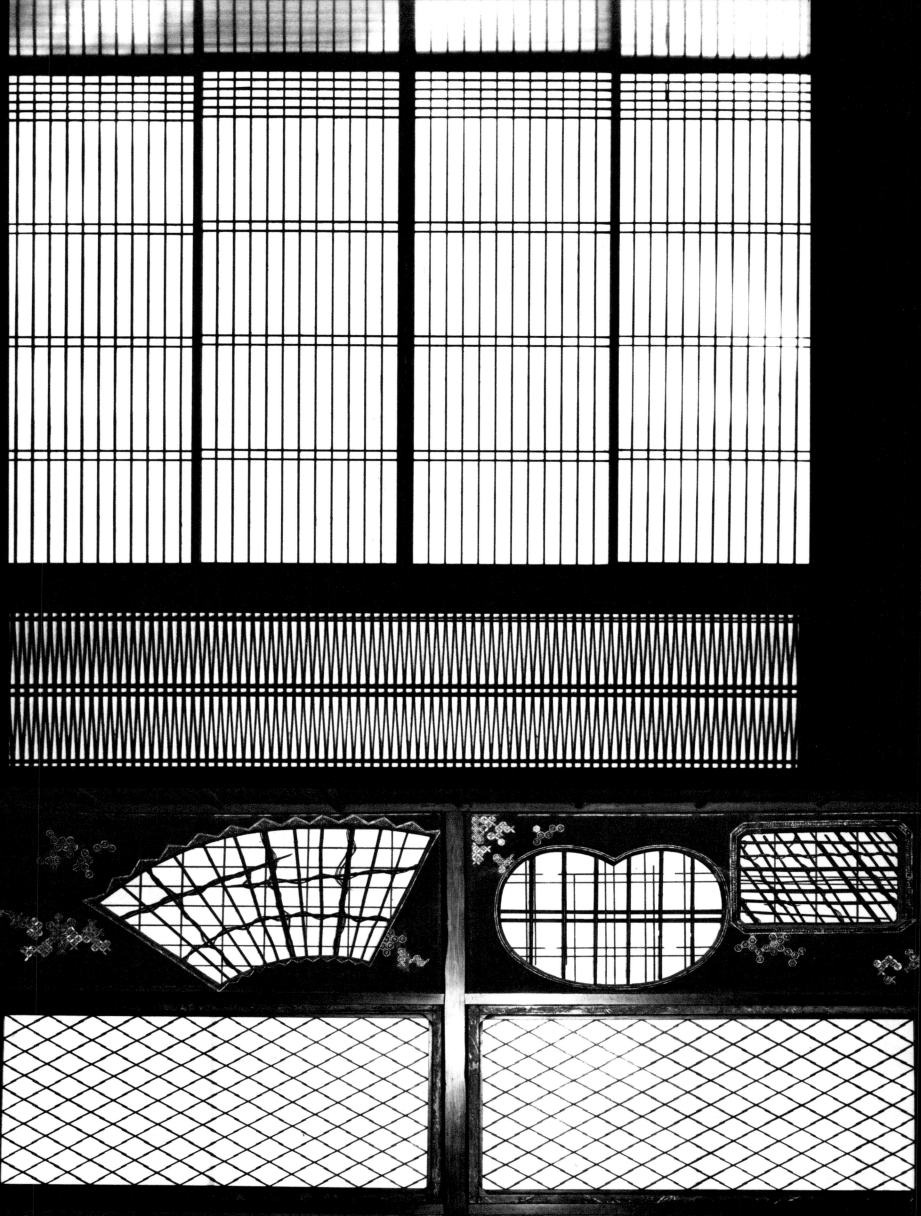

飛騨の君山

子孫長久
生業繁榮

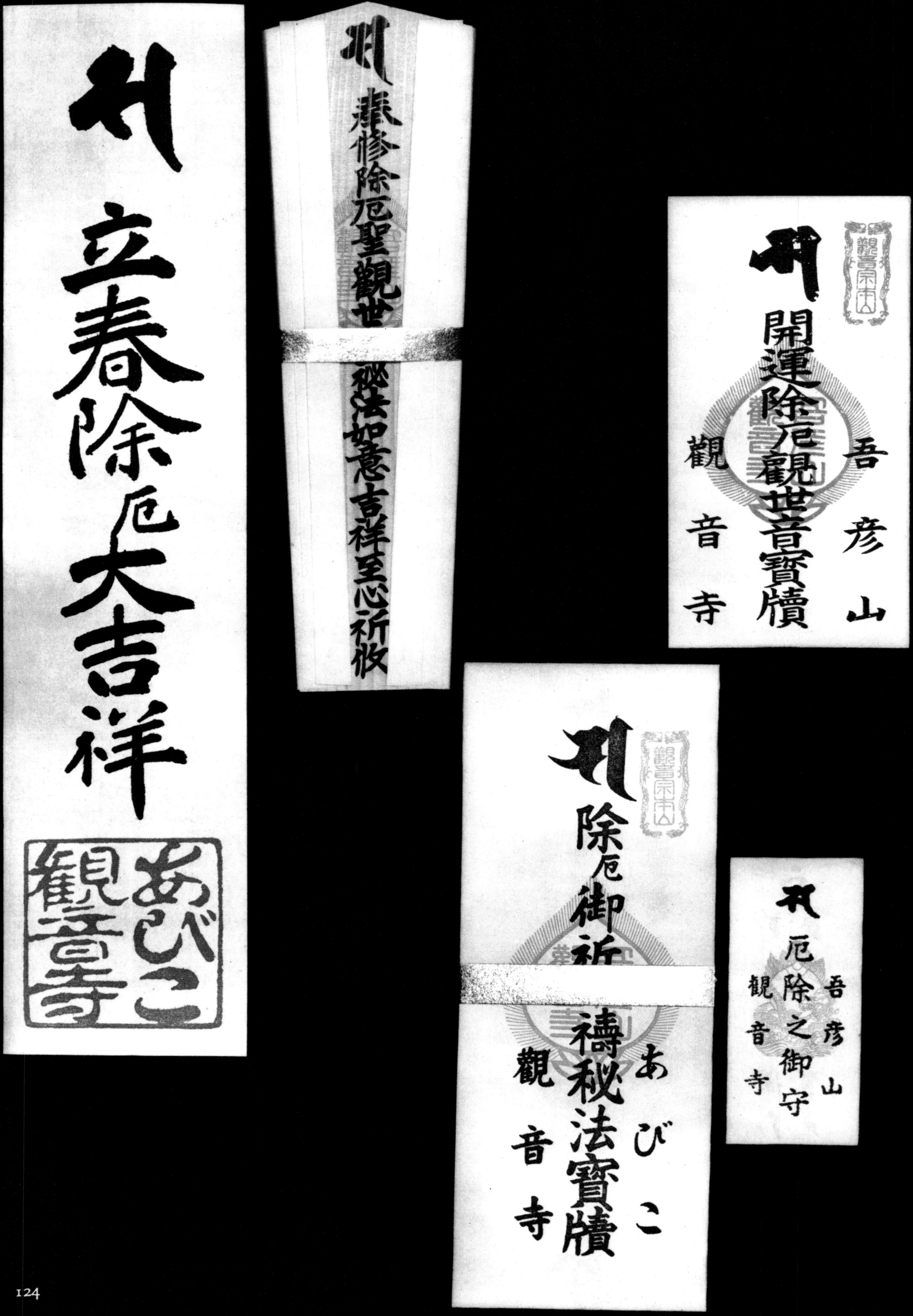

ब

立春除厄大吉祥

あびこ観音寺

春修除厄聖観世秘法如意吉祥至心祈攸

ब 開運除厄觀世音寶牘

吾彦山 觀音寺

ब 除厄御祈禱秘法寶牘

あびこ 觀音寺

ब 厄除之御守

吾彦山 観音寺

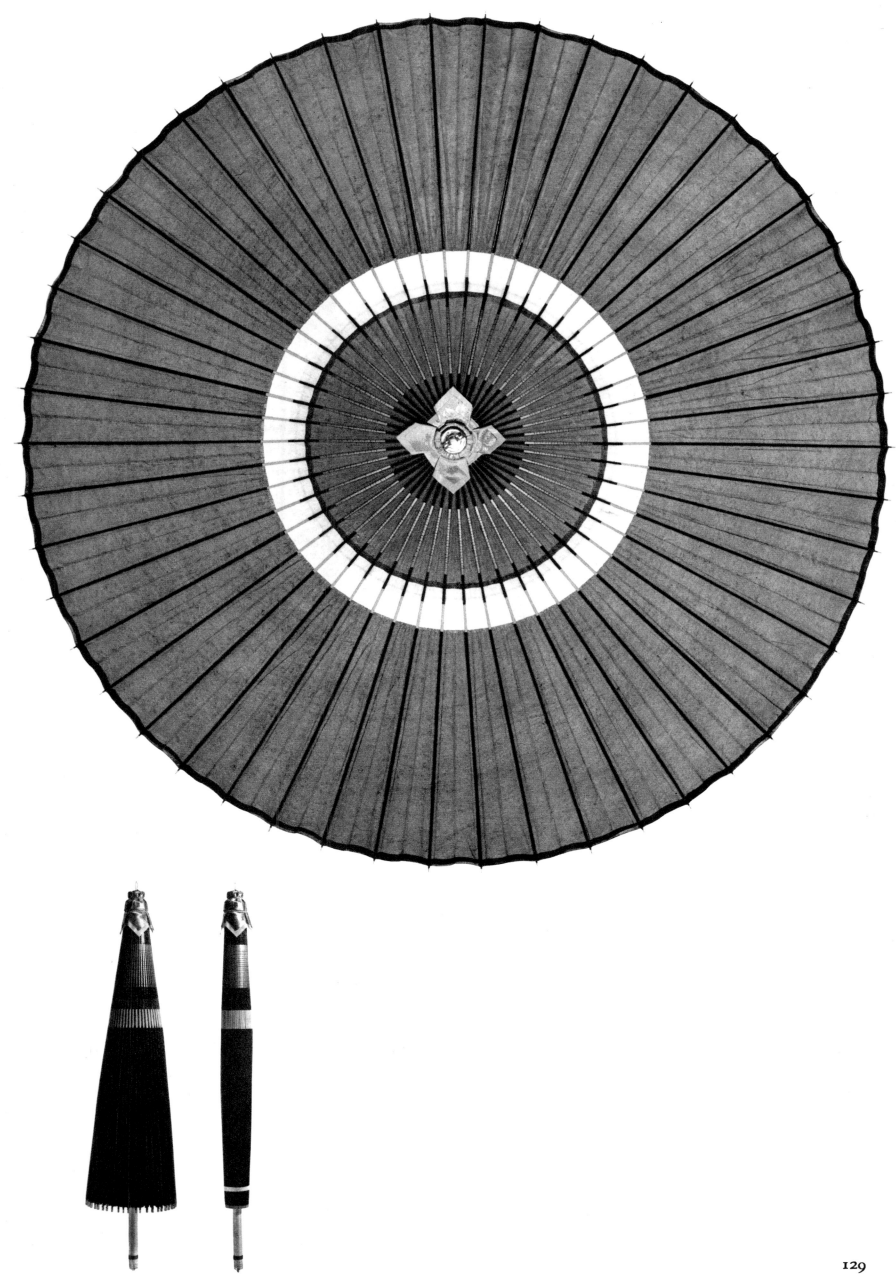

129

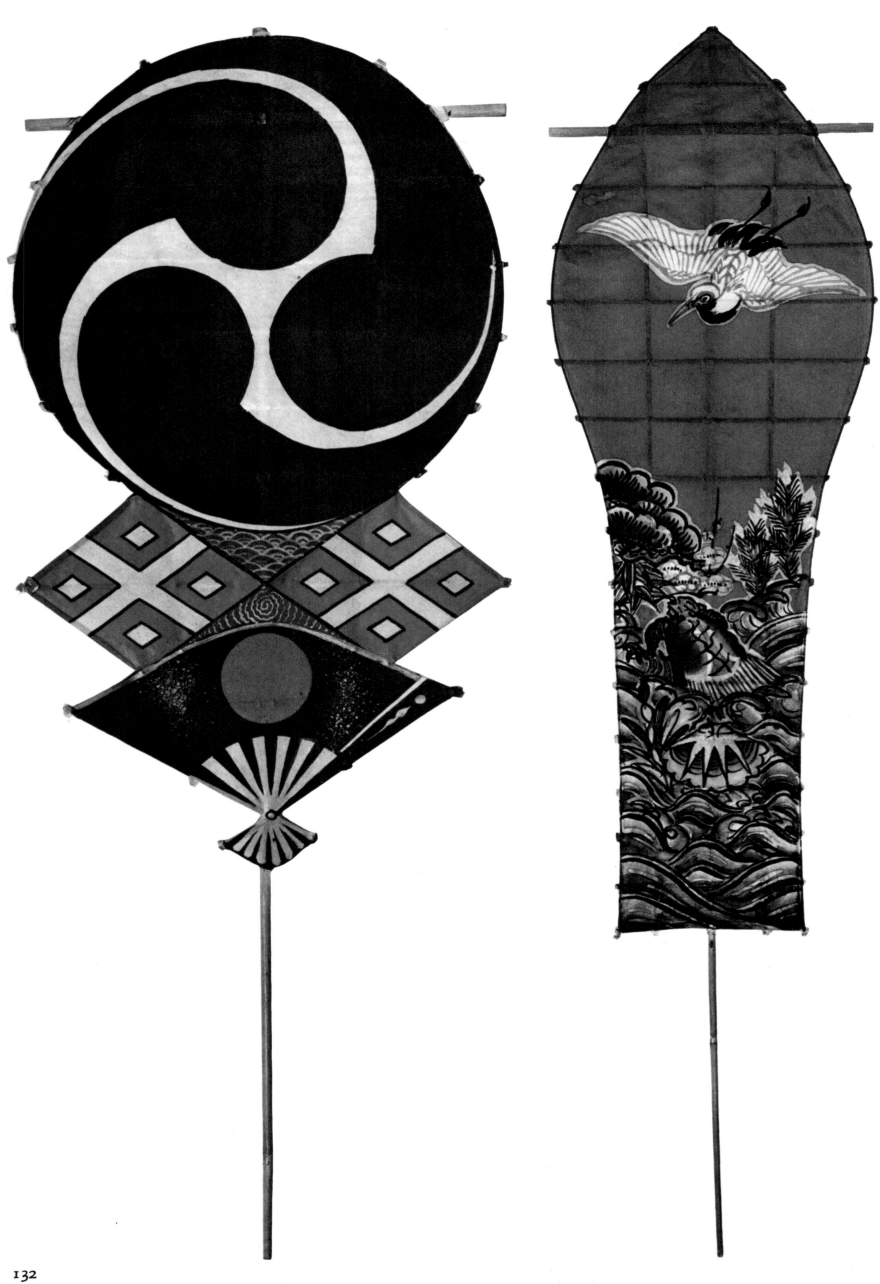

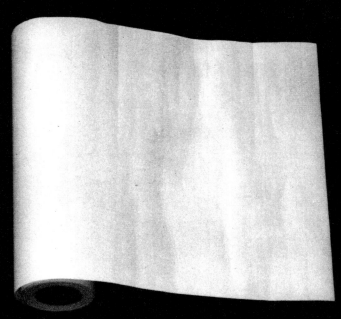

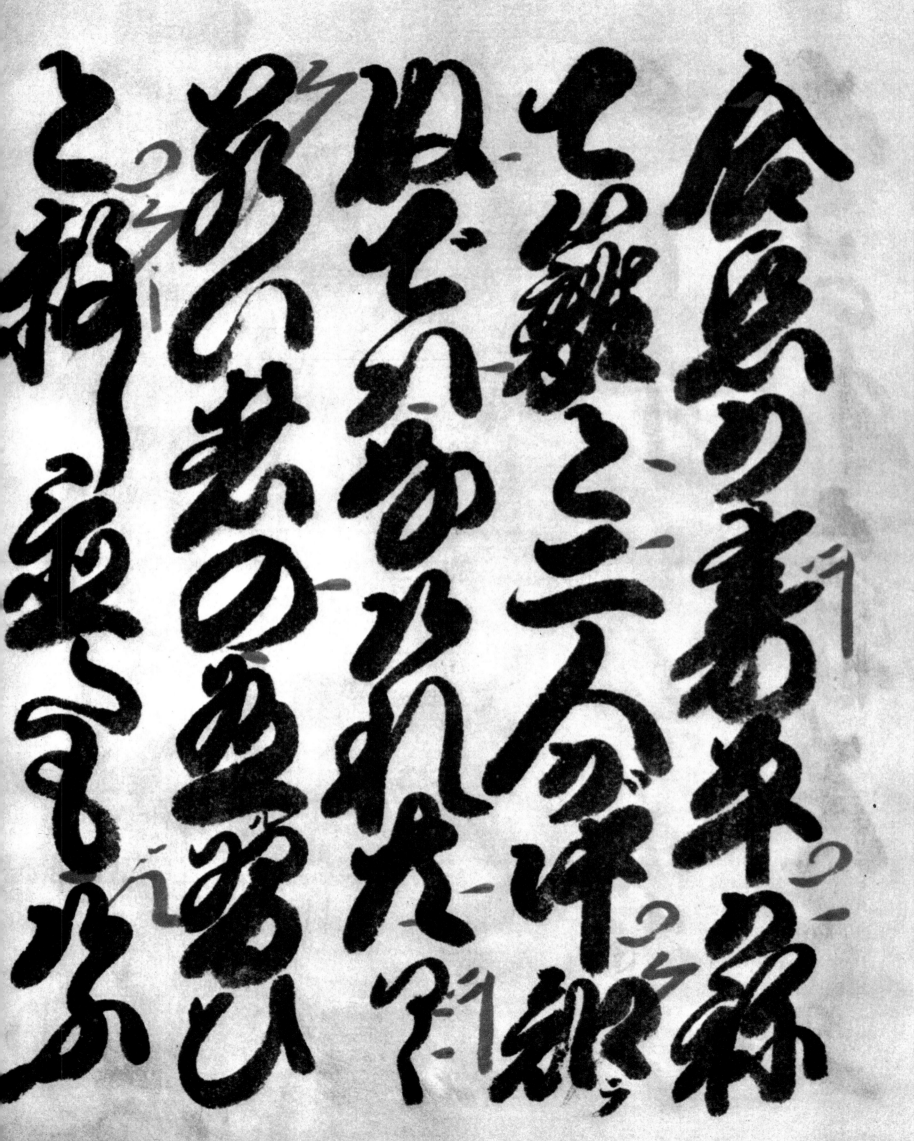

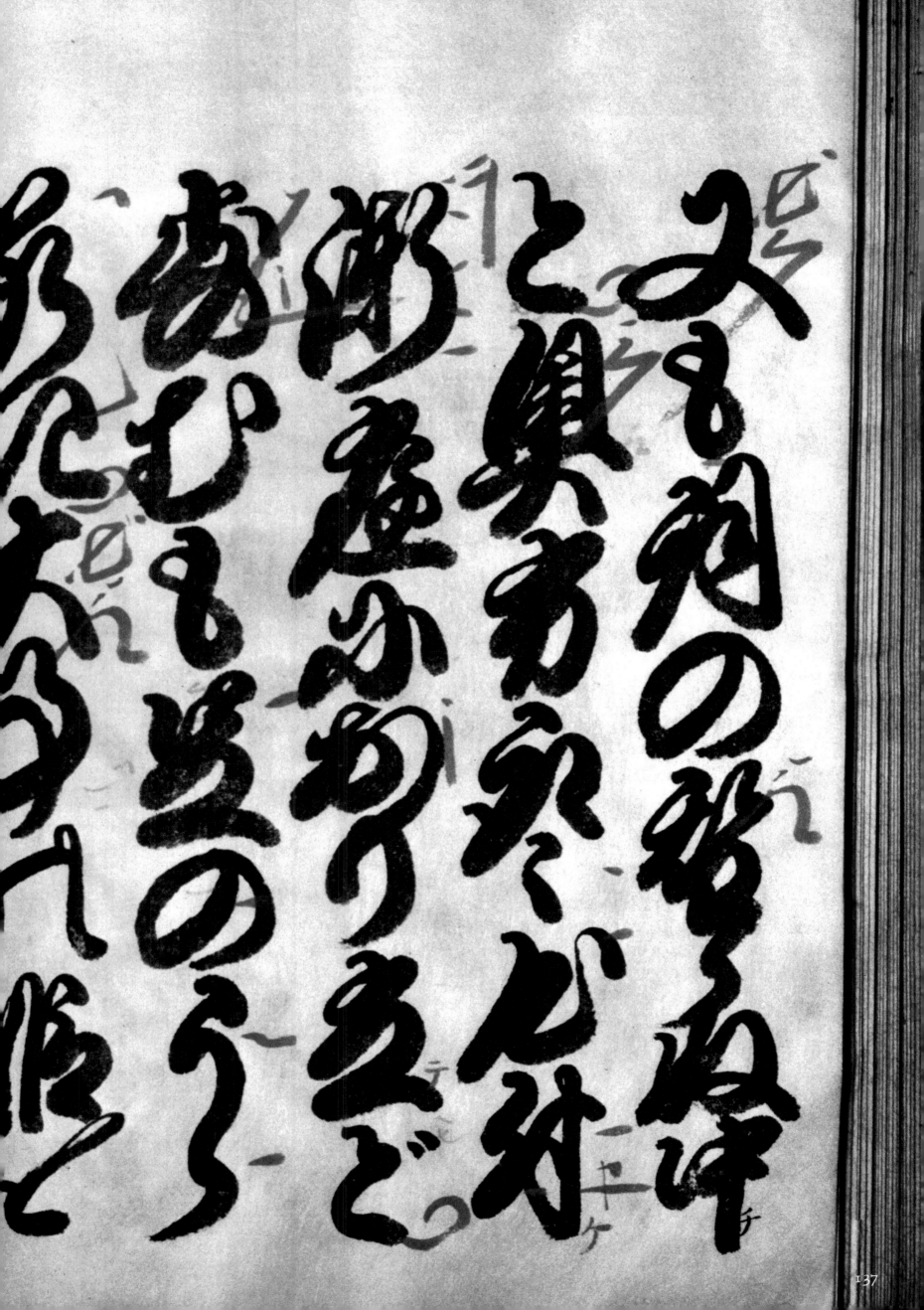

清元流正本　第貳編

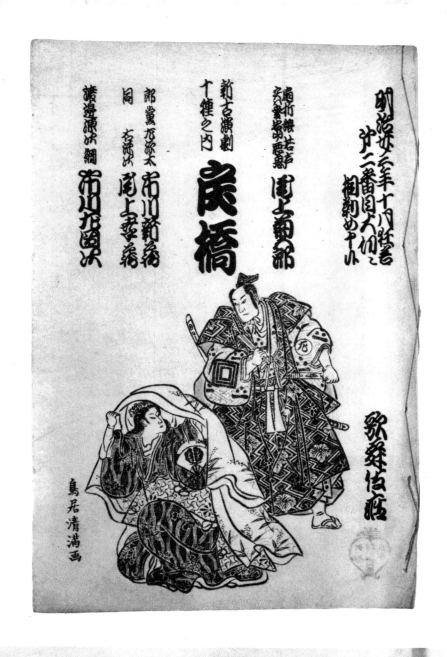

右常磐津一流太夫直傳之正本者私方ヨリ外ニ決而無御座
仍而太夫自筆ヲ取而節章句ヲ正シ
令開版者也御求御覧被遊可被下候以上

常磐津小文字太夫
常磐津大文字太夫
常磐津組太夫

岸澤式佐
岸澤三藏
岸澤三八

同松尾太夫　三弦
同真砂太夫
同家佐太夫　三弦

常磐津正本版元
印刷兼發行者
坂川平四郎

東京都台東區谷中清水町壱番地

天保九戌霜月
昭和廿三年一月再版

うつぼ下五丁

（坂川藏版）

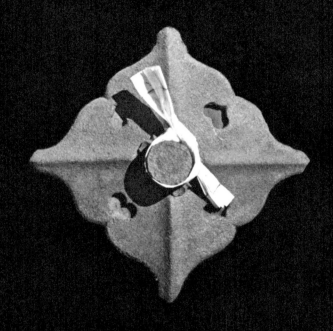

土

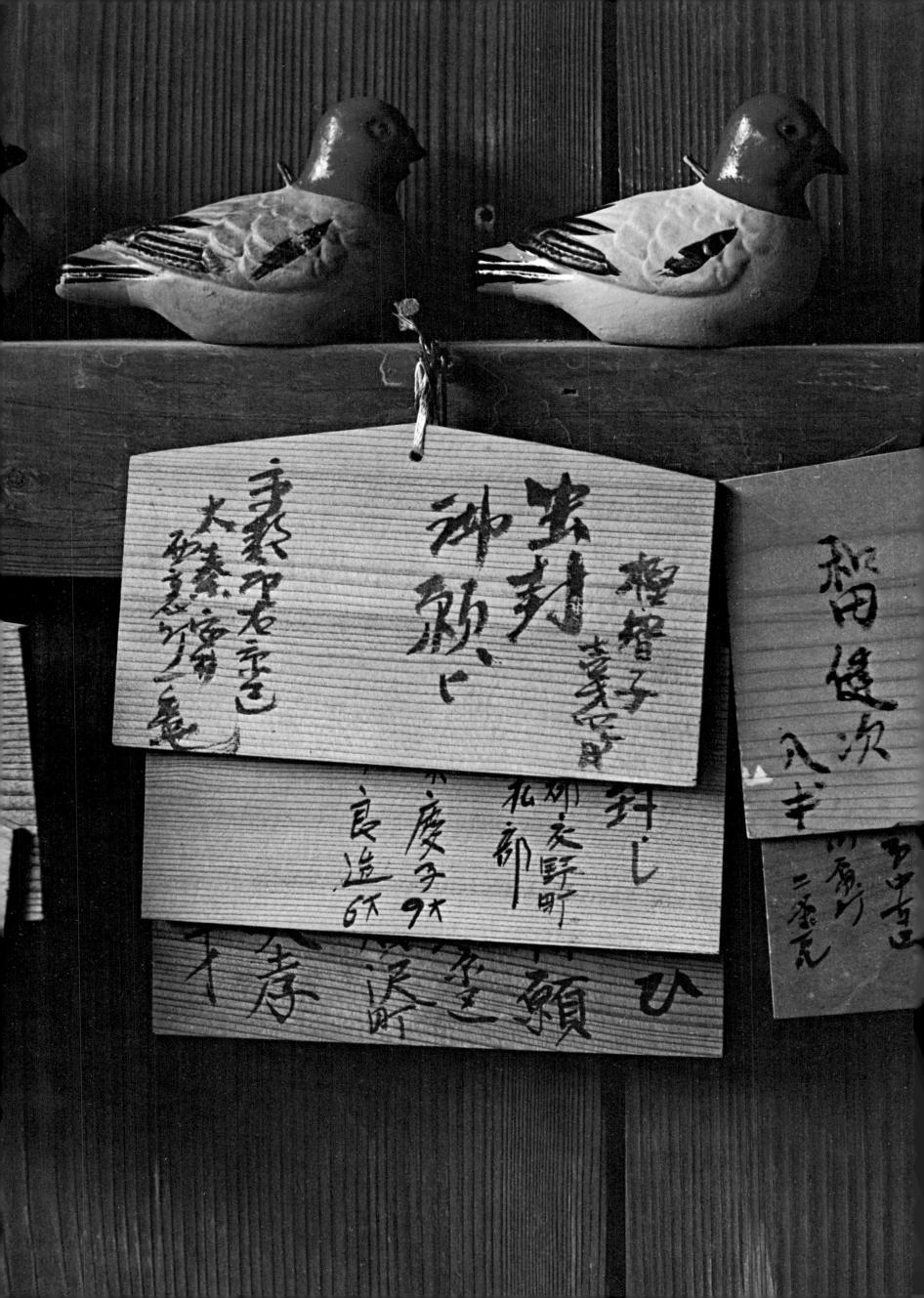

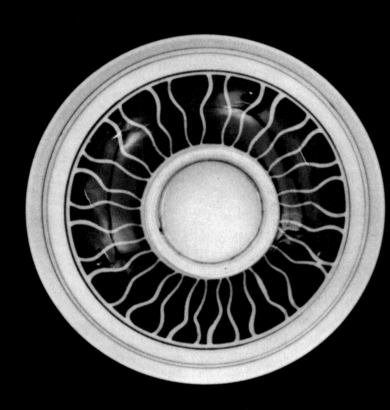
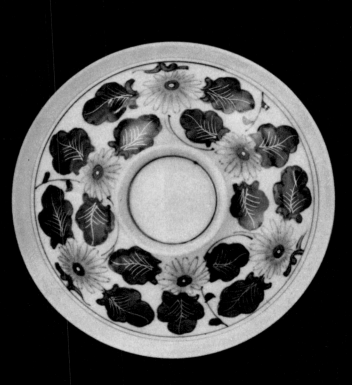
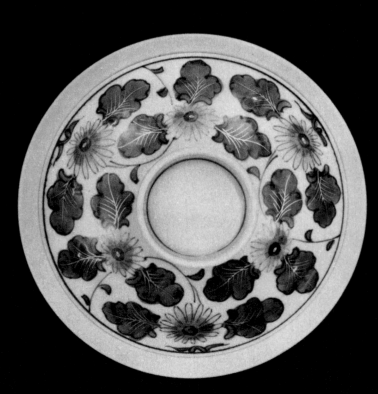

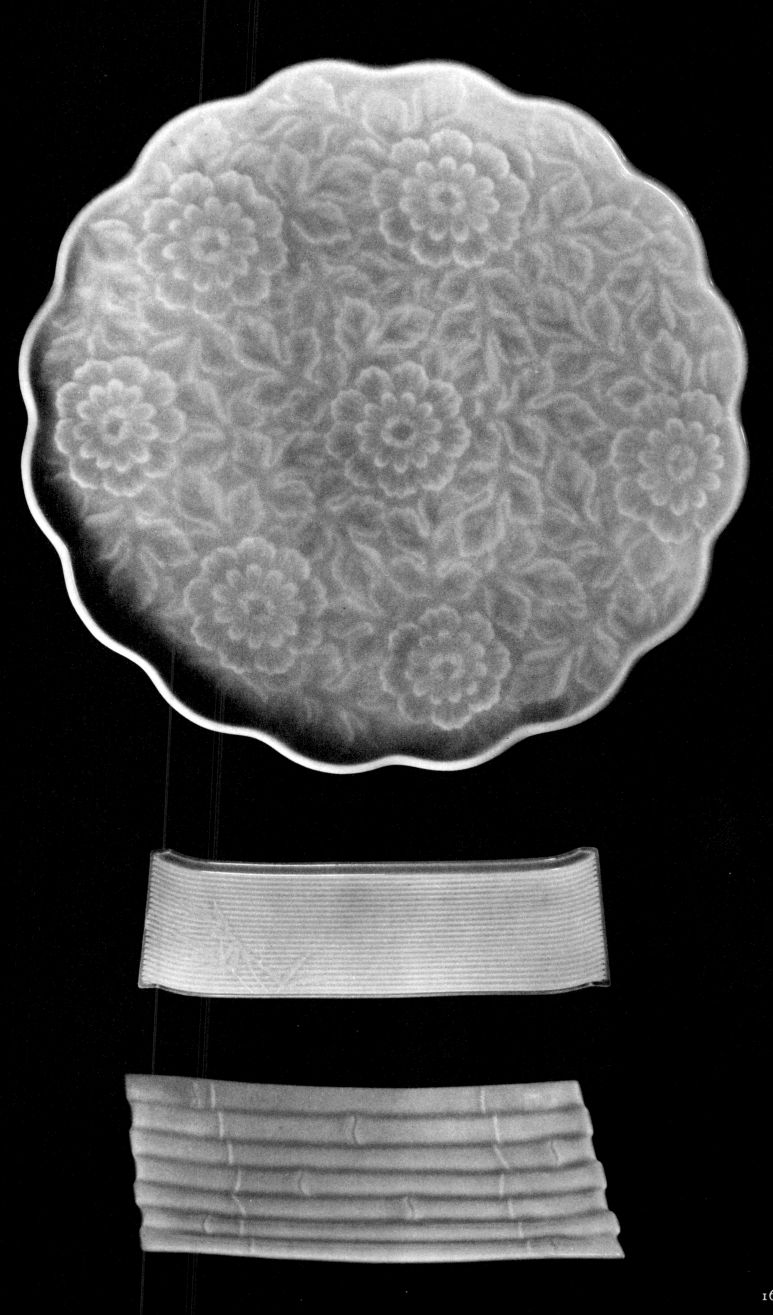

Date Due